ON WINGS OF SOUND

ON WINGS OF SOUND

An Autobiographical Story in Poetry, 1968-1980

Stella Browning

Illustrated by
Roland Portchmouth

Foreword by
Allison Nichols Johnn-St. Johnn, Ph.D.

To ALLISON
with dearest love

Always

My world would stand but still—
   and lie
Had I the power lost to choose
   and sigh—
Ply with the violin but wondering—
   to sigh
To cry: given the power of age
   wherein
Tempo is never lost—
                Eternity within:
Then teach me Thy way of strings
            with mystery
              echoing
       the wings of sound . . .

October 26, 1980

FIRST EDITION

© 1983 by Stella Browning

ISBN 0 946622 00 0

Printed in the United States of America
by
Exposition Press, Inc.
325 Rabro Drive
Smithtown, NY 11787-0817

DEDICATED TO MY ANCESTRAL TOWN

An Easter Crystal

—April—

The crystal softly lapping edge
Each wave a miniature that rests
For moment as a thought to pledge

One oyster-catcher views this vast stage
A gleaming strand where rival birds sand-press
At the crystal softly lapping edge

Where sand-martins as courtiers arrange
Then wade with hop, a-wing fruitless
For moment as a thought to pledge

The migratory sandpiper head-nodding on ledge
The lapwing graceful with fine long crest
At the crystal softly lapping edge

Sand golden mile bordered with bank and sedge
Nests like darkness concealed, artless
For moment as a thought to pledge

All morning thrusts with burst of winged cortège
The laughing gull with an Easter sunburst rests
At the crystal softly lapping edge
For moment as a thought to pledge.

New Romney.

Published by Dr. John Tapia in *Now* magazine, *Durango Herald,* April 29, 1982. Poems from "Romney Marsh Tapestry" in appreciation and the invocation of God's Blessing in the work for Peace received from Pope John Paul II to the Author 13:4:83 from Vatican.

Contents

List of Illustrations

"*An Easter Crystal.*" The village as it was before World War II
"*Of Romney Marsh.*" Wildlife, beach winding 'round Dungeness, sand, dunes, pebbles, sea wall, sealane, ships, sea wind, marsh grass
"*Key to the Dawn.*" Eagle, eerie road in sun, hilltops, sunburst, loch, sheen, heron
"*Reality in Vision.*" God took my hand, cloud rising from the mountains
"*White Crests of Iona.*" Giant waves tumbling, guillemôt, tidal race, wind, wave on wave, rippled sand, starred machair, abbey
"*At the Calf Sales.*" Small ring, Highland calf, auctioneer, beer drinker, tweeds, cows, circle of bidders railing the ring, smokers, smoke, farmer's sticks; tartan tammy, finger poised
"*Breach Birth.*" Crossing of the *Minch* to Barra, waters boiling over, curled with surge, leaping wave, toiling ship, motion, spume, wretching sides, missile rains
"*Ormistons.*" The Poltalloch Estate (photograph by the late Col. Lord George Malcolm of Duntrune Castle)
"*An April Sea Symphony.*" "Under the shadow of Thy wings will I rejoice" (Psalm 63)
"*Bouquêt in Glendaruel.*" Grasses, winds, stream, heather, marguerites, buttercups, daisies, hedgerow, bracken's brae
"*Old Men Within Blue Grass.*" Coal tips, door-to-door street, stooping men, coalmine dirt, women with shopping basket, the local, smoke-tired sky, the silent men
"*You Are Walking in My Shadow.*" My shadow, fair head, towering fir, laced elms, woods
"*To My Grandchildren.*" Children's faces, wine glass tipped as wine flows, grapes, lemons, apples, apple blossom, linen
"*In Guadeloupe I Pick a Flower.*" Lava's lips, earth's steaming bowel, rock, rain forest, set of sun, lonely feeling
"*Christmas Dawns on Romney Marsh.*" Norman cloistered prayers, mullioned window, shaft of light
"*At Wesley.*" Nature's pattern, roses, holly, sycamore, robin, other garden flowers
"*The Overcoat Man.*" Scottish sunrise, ball of fire, river, wood, hilltop, overcoat man, tea, leafed branch
"*An Introduction to Oak House.*" From a sketch by Guy Dearlove
"*On Wings of Sound.*" Foam ballerina's dance, coils and plumes of cloud, gulls, billowed tide, curtain of rain, sunbeams

Illustrations by the Reverend Mr. Roland J. Portchmouth, N.D.D., A.T.D., 1978, Strathtay, Perthshire PH9 OPG.

The Reverend also illustrated the Children's Educational Books by the author: *Butter in the Buttercups* (parts 1, 2, and 3), *Notail at Wesley* with the Winter Sequence of *Butter in the Buttercups*, and *The Adventures of Hoodie the Crow.*

ix

Foreword

On Wings of Sound? Or *Stella Browning?* Both. The two are one, for the magnificent volume, *On Wings of Sound,* is a remarkable twelve-year achievement autobiography. It is unusual, each subject or moment having been written when the author's joys, tears, laughter, or sighs were still fresh and warm with life and now still sounding as if from the chords of a great organ and the tremblings of strings in the distance playing the echoes.

It seems that Stella Browning is especially gifted in writing true stories or happenings in verse. A striking example is seen in one of her recent, most interesting and pleasing works, *Butter in the Buttercups,* a story for and of children and life of the woodlands, but the high and consistent literary quality of the book stamps it also a treasure for adults, indeed, a classic. However, in the beauty, truth, and fine poetic mastery of this autobiography, the author has excelled herself.

To read *On Wings of Sound* lures one to read and reread it many times, absorbing, enjoying, and appreciating its life pulsations from the heart of the poet, whose each heartbeat pulsates ever with it, each poem inviting and exciting adventure. From the prologue, "The Loom of Sound," the vivid pictures pass, each painting and imprinting indelibly its own heartbeat; "Mull of Kintyre," "The Red Admiral," on and on, each verse accompanied by its intrinsic notes or faithful acknowledgments, on to the grand finale, "On Wings of Sound," the title poem, commanding and crowning its unique and protected place in the poetry of today and today's life in literature. Superb beauty of expression, every essential and form required of all true poetry are present. The making of a poet, a favorite consideration and often a near-general concept, does have its place. However, with Stella Browning a poet was *born* and the "making" in-depth. Her ability increased, her understanding increased, her knowledge increased, but today's result was implanted in the seed. Stella Browning's writings are alive, living, can be felt and absorbed. The nuances, tone colors, soft or strong, with their clear imageries in fitting rhythmical expression, are ever in evidence.

Miss Browning was born in 1917 in New Romney, Kent, England, and is now living in the house in which she was born. Today she is one of the most talented, interesting, and prolific of contemporary bards. She was graduated from London University with honors in French and psychology, afterward attending a finishing school in France. Her writing began at a very early age, but her father, being rather somewhat Victorian, discouraged the activity believing that a woman's place was not to be a writer. The daughter yielded, casting aside (apparently) her gifted bent for writing. But Time moves on and Life strikes with its gray and grayer to dark color tones in everyone's days, yet one day Light pierces and penetrates every and any horizon, destroying the ominous shades bringing to Life its joyous fulfillments.

One day Stella Browning wrote again. During somewhat difficult periods, she spent much time in Scotland, where many of her most beautiful and cherished poems were written, and upon her return to England her remarkable writing career really began. Well travelled and well known in English poetry circles and organizations, Miss Browning is founder and editor of the Cinque Ports Poets Society, and is listed in *Who's Who in the World* (1978-1981) and in several other notable international biographies. In addition to her books of poetry (among which I mention *Pilgrimage, Butter in the Buttercups, The Adventures of Hoodie the Crow,* and *Notail at Wesley)* published in England and America, articles and other writings published under a pseudonym, she is also a popular lecturer and recently had signed a contract with the British Broadcasting Corporation for poetry readings of her work in Introduction to Schools in the British Isles.

Stella Browning, a Fellow of Cambridge Academy of Poets and of the International Biographical Association, has been awarded many Certificates of Merit, appears in the international *Who's. Who in Poetry* for "Distinguished Contribution to Poetry," and received other numerous prizes of high significance.

> *On Wings of Sound!* Its voice
> Echoing its *living* song in tones of
> Beauty's chords of quintessence . . .
> The book and its author, a delightful two,
> A complete and exceptional . . . *one!*

Allison Nichols Johnn-St. Johnn, Ph.D.
Author, Editor, Literary Consultant
New York, New York

Author's Preface

This collection was formed over a period of the last twelve years. Certain poems link the chain from the success of *Pilgrimage and Other Poems* in 1972, with their addition now as important in retrospect from renewed knowledge and awareness in the true vision extended in belief, in stimulation of that awareness, with its truly wider aspect on life in diversity and adversity within oneself and the joys of sharing all great and wonderful things with others.

Poems, therefore, through this experience have found their place with further awards and publications. Precious and concise thoughts have materialized in a wider vision since *Pilgrimage,* and the works here contained are a complete spiritual gain, in a sense a second *Pilgrimage*! Nature the healer of all wounds—"Harvest," the finalization of the essence of Life—from divorce to remarriage and:

"Under the shadow of Thy wings will I rejoice." (Psalm 63)

Prologue

The Loom of Sound

Not till the loom is silent
   and the shuttles cease to fly
shall God unroll the canvas
   to explain the reason why
how each dark thread is needful
   in the Weaver's skillful hands
as the threads of gold and silver
   in the pattern He has planned?
This morning's skies are clover
   with my valentine in His hand,
my solitary prayers are answered
        —Now that I understand—

Thought taken from 1 Cor. 13:12—" . . . then shall I know . . ."

1

Milestones

Should we look my love to another shore
Or count our blessings by the score?
Why must this cup of happiness o'erflow
When time is forbidding, our endless foe?

We seek and find, heaven-sent our gain,
Would it be such love could wane?
Dear heart, such sorrow could not rest
In the confusion of my breast.

Cross strings and bows but not our heart
This death knell call for we could not part?
The will still to climb . . . are we never there?
Yes, with God-given strength, a rest, and a prayer.

Published in *Poetry Cavalcade,* 1971.

The first poem written since childhood in 1970. The first poem written at age nine, "Crocus Beds," won the award of a complete set of Dickens.

Of Romney Marsh

Fragrance of a salt marsh cradles—
rocks every winding lane, stabilizes mile on mile
    where dropping of a memory spells
Instinct picked up by well-worn key: lifts the thatching
                   Wide
on her quick peace . . . Wild life cries free—

Sweep of a vast marsh plain pillows a dream: visions
                      Clear
Could I forget a maroon fission ochre sky?
    Horizon of wild fowl rush, hollow nest
and the beach winds lithesome arms around Dungeness,
                  Holds
World-anchored, sea-lane ships
in vivid greens, flat marsh uplifted to her pebbled breast:

Where the marsh grass dry thistled high
so I long-tangled, laughed—cried! Crawled bare of knee
    with beach and gun: Lambs still rest,
guest with gorse, bask in cleave of sun!
Mellow odors of bread baking: cakes, rabbit pie making
    an evening's mist ridden and outwon.

Where sweet freedom flies and marsh soul receives Communion
and the sea wind waves a salt Union Jack
over a newly populated, broad-acred dominion.

From Romney: her Norman steepled spires,
her whispering whistling telegraph wires, golden sands
    wed to dunes with shrimp-pink beds:
Shells pearl of swan journeying on—Moon
              Harvest red—
rushed, tumbled August on feathered stairs,
blue-black mirrored lake bleak from freshly ditched beach . . .
    a rest of winged curlew chorus stirs fair:

On water wings I tide
    a green-breakered surf-sweeping
        long-billowed ride—
            and my ecstasy flows
                sand-seeps and re-glows . . .

Where the Good Lord gave GREENER GRASS GROWS!
Marsh men saved their silt land; dykes, seawall's teeth
firmly ground.
On dark minstrel starred nights where an oaken laugh rings
hearts breathe a soft fire, cheerfully sing—
swing a thin shepherd's crook—curved ghost of a smuggler's
brandy-pink grin!

From beamed meadows the Cinque Port of New Romney
steals:
curves, wings gently as dunlins—swallows quiet
and teals—
her church bells as soft, pleasant descant ring her appeal . . .

In London awards, 1971. Published in *Pilgrimage*, 1972, judged by John Smith, editor, *Poetry Review:* "highly commended." Published in *Horizon,* 1974. Watford *Observer,* 1972, in article; reviewed by June Chisholm.

Written in retrospect at Oban. New Romney, town of my birth; one son born in New Romney now living in San José; eldest born at Capel-le-Fern and living at Hertfordshire.

As Sweet Breath*

(On return from Majorca)

Warm in their own Creation
  of a world poignant,   young as the day
Flower as the lemon tree   in warm folded air
  hungry as scent,   yet delicate

                As Camellias

Fragile this bright moment of blossoming care:
caress winged as a butterfly   First petals of love
  folds triumph of Spring   in soft touch of kiss,
Hand-twine as honeysuckle   moistening of lips
  breast tipped as roses   perfumed,
    bruised   as all Creation
    in tangle of arms   Limbs which triumph
as fair wisteria coils   flesh-pink spring among

                Dark

toiling leaves   flowers and fruit are
  the riches love leaves,   sprays first real emotion
           the tight bunch
          —BOUQUÊT—

Massed armfuls of roses that pattern our cross
  still Youth's beautiful day   Azalea who bears
    her flowers fragrant   Alone
          Thorn when born

Both protective and piercing where stream of blood flows
         engulfing the richness
        —SWEET BREATH—

Even in aging the separate   may gather the rose?
  fruit which has fallen   Love then too much
    the bittersweet   the dry husk?

*The poem may be read from left to right across, also left- and right-hand columns separately.

Written in 1967. Published in *Pilgrimage,* 1972; chosen by John Smith.

A first "breath" for many years of foreign shores since childhood in Loire Valley.

6

On Leaving One's Friends

When all the sticks and stones are packed
  Address to friends in gilt-edged piled
Goodbyes are tied with surety around life
  With friends old who share our joy with strife!
Golden years know the move maybe
  Almost like paying a penalty?
Around a corner unknown know
  Indifferent stranger—a friend—foe?

Let sunshine into doubt fragment
  A refreshing smile welcome raiment
To stranger, your calmer heart refresh
  The unknown friend of path now newly
                        Blest.

Riches

With gray head bent low o'er parcelled care
  Then raised eyes brimful meet mine in dull despair:
To lose in small clasped purse: her all—
  In bleak early morning cold has no power to recall
Just where or when the loss but to her senses tragical!

A long search in vain where no favors sought . . .
  For greater loss is when there is NO response, doubt
In the fullness of living, how comfort was my gain!
  To cheer, to hear her solitary fears, to call me
                  —Friend—
We sat where only God could hear, a Kingdom in the name.

No pence could buy, false love cannot tie
Friendship's knot, only the shared feeling to rely . . .
  No hand hot with riches—but full of all joy—
  In sharing of burden! To leave always behind

Gladness within another's heart links our own peace of mind.

1968, Watford.

1970, Oban. The first experience of "Stranger" when living in Oban. The distress of the stranger who had lost her purse with no money to return to the Isles.

7

Sole Wanderings of Her Naked Feet
(The birth of my granddaughter, Julia)

PULSED FAIR as the engaged morning
   —JULIA, child asleep—
Loved as to a loving woman born
in her innocence from October's wind
    where hatred never enters mind;
    the bud unfolds its silks in kind
of gift-whorled petal fold to sepal

    where hearts must learn

         A CHILD ASLEEP
—will she be worn, will—torn?—
The silk in flower blossom again:
rain in a time to rise, bear again pain
    in birth, the drive of her own green
    from flower's sprayed warmth within—
Her time to close petalled eyes in sleep

    from flourish of her beauteous inner self:

         A CHILD ASLEEP
—this palace dwells within her heart!
Where the dear secret heart must learn.
O hard hearts must learn to realize
    time, when flowers the velvet
    share of bed; platonic in new age?
Marriage? Curls sweet fame?

    Close brimming eyes from silks and satin

Sheets of content,
—riches to rags again?—
Her essence in a maidenhead of dreams
Pulsed fair as the engaged morning:
    woman with child
    blown-wild blossoms free—proud innocence!
In sole wanderings of her naked feet

    Crown JULIA, child asleep

1968. Julia is my granddaughter, born while I was in exile in Scotland. Now one of the two *Buttercups* children of the Children's Educational verses, published in 1977.

8

Crept a Small Craft with a Twinkling Oar

Crept a small craft with a twinkling oar
  black mirrored pool of harbors
    jet with olive:

a ring of cool water marries to the Bay
  with joy I sketch along gray shore
    swan-cool as yesterday's

Promenade polish of hard snow and sway
  My small craft with a twinkling oar:
    jet spiral before

Today's moments stretched before the fire—
  my sail, canvas of fifty summers' queue
    as herring gull on windowsill
      for more:
Rocking chair dreams in roll of pastures new—
  I hear a shout—the roar—
  unsteady feet sweep me upon the quay

Giant wave jet-swept
      to marry this small craft
        with an unsure
          twinkling oar.

For Robin

On early winter's path
   A whimbrel rippling cries—
winged morning aviary
   where swift joins the bonny heather
pairs of pigeon, tern replies . . .
   and coverts where white frosted crumbs
secretly disguise

across winter's icy path
   again we surely meet;
this time I cannot traverse
   where your wee feet
alight, cling to the rink of tiles,
   exchange a vivid commentary
with bewitched, chilled sparrows' whiles:

Drift winter's woollen paths
   her spinning loom of eaves;
the hoot of owl flakes from nights
   white rigors . . . eerie leaves . . .
Shrill scream of gull
   and robin wakes: trills—vigorous
Tomato red around my windowsill!

   A crumb for robin
     long blest
King's nature's festooned aviary
     of crows where wild winter
beaks I quench and fill!

Oban, 1970.

Both poems written in the same week while staying with my cousin.

"For Robin" published in *Pilgrimage,* 1972.

Twenty Moments in Blindness

The Cloak of Jacob

I awaken in dawn when night's insight remains—
Curious silence where the spirit only speaks
asks not for quiet but LIGHT . . .
a cold-sweat panic churns the mist
grays range, blacks change in still mass
to gravitate on a beaded plain
            drops
                Soul
from wells deeper spell of darkness
where feint faith climbs, shares divided hell
in a falling chilled knowledge knowing NOW
how minutes only chain this lifeline!

Mind crawls as a serpent: winds, coils, hisses
in mist where spit has stayed the tongue:
saliva quivers sprayed dry on air
hammers my heart appalled in fear:
I fall—upon a cotton-reel?
How small—at edge of precipice
            I kneel
                as oil
masks water in a liquid haze
intense divining gray to white—interchange
in sheer pain of eyes on fire—
this constant still-white grave

O please the sight of opening door!
Mind pours; swimming in seas of unknown home,
rain-beats as skeleton's knock on windowpanes—
feeling each droplet yet to come
in waiting, crouching, stealing along
a peninsular hard floor
            A shadow dim?
            I stumble—
Pilgrim rise as arcs my Soul from blinded eyes—
Surely clearer vision; truant, now appears?
O Darkness with severity is flown—
Gone, swept as a stone—yet, unlike a fall of
            Pebble drops,

a bottomless
deep well

My vision clearly, yes, serenely finds
God's treasury in sight's recovery
the certain wisdom held by blind!
In given strength this Cloak of Jacob veils—
Yet wrapped as sheath when pitch of understanding
pales . . .
—The Wings of Sound—

The poem recounts the momentary blindness brought on by anxiety and
through the experience a richer fullness in living. It expresses the treasure
of sight which until then had been taken for granted. A new window to
the world . . .

Symmetry

Into this calm . . .
and certain way of palette sea, deep azure blue
scales silver candled stars in swift, iridescent
      light
a tabernacle paints by mystic Hand
and sweeps the brush to mauve nocturnal hills
      this land
that smiles in dipped shadows of Divine right!
From chariot wheels gray clouds a plume of
      "horse-tails"
drifting white, the canvas breathes
and from a murmur in a rippled dream one sees
      the neap of Tide
from quietness as limpets munch
      in the deep weed . . .

Soft opal light transforms the lips of waves,
      pipe of lone gull on high flute notes
piercing Heaven's steadfastness, O welcome night,
as Death sans fear one HEARS the turn of tide?
      The grave is sweet
where hills are symmetry of buried charcoal fires
Into this calm . . .

Oban Bay. Published in *Poetry Panorama,* 1971.

The renewal of faith with the transmission of light. Life as the "nocturnal hills" again forms its symmetry . . .

Key to the Dawn

Oban to Loch Earne

Faith in His existence turns the key
when sheep, hawk, and solitary man are one
where golden eagle treads an eerie road in sun;

breached rivers, hilltops new are ours to wind
where morning sunbursts on loch's frosted frond
where hare's waxen trance on horseshoe roads shine

where silence melts as ice from dark soft-keyed
where Faith when whipped from gray silken sheen
as fish beneath the answering wings of heron!

Published in *Envoi,* 1977: "superb final stanza, very evocative," P. Berlyer.

Concentration upon the words "where there is doubt sow Faith"—St. Francis
of Assisi's Prayer.

A Prayer

Dear Lord,
Give courage for untrammelled ways
For love though constant not our lips to praise:
To show Thy mercy in those endless, countless days.

Give courage
To spend nights wrought with loneliness, despair,
Feel yet again the morning sun, to care
That each day may dawn serene; to mock me, fair?

Blessing
Hearts filled with pain, tortured and seeing not the snare
Of unspoken word, false lips that share
Not our solitude and leave us to the world devoid of love
        yet voiced in Prayer.

Published in *Poetry Zodiac,* 1971.

Written before packing a sleeping bag to spend the following "Night above
a thousand feet" . . .

Night Above a Thousand Feet

The Question

1969

to curl beneath the pink blanket of sunset
 a Kingdom in a twilight smile
across sweet Heaven's lips fair press
 on mine:

into lifted rippled laughter
 in revelry of velvet rainbow sky
and far musical water
 to believe

is then to question why?
 to wonder, to glory, does Life die
Stranger to tears?
 In dusk of lost words

for beauties Hand with morning's sorrow
 Crowns each good-bye
The flood of weeping cloud comes after
 when weather howls

This sad, radiant embrace
 has massed in midnight, glows
bows to the supreme Hand of Time . . .
 as breathless
 dawn grips mine . . .

Published in *Pilgrimage,* 1972. Used in lecture with the second poem, "The Answer." Poems read in Oban Cathedral and Iona Abbey.

Written in the dawn from a night spent in sleeping bag at Arrochar, Scotland. On the return from the "Cobbler" peak, 1,011 feet.

Reality in Vision

The Answer

1970

above three thousand feet
and when God took my hand
     I cried . . .

no Vision this His breath
I felt beside:
     where cloud

in Truth's moment lies
within its own frail,
     sweet loveliness

the hidden Hand holds me
in its grave and tenderness—
     birdlike poised

Winged in a morning's cage!
Within another breath
     slowly cloud

outrode its own white gossamer
mist, as Death disappears,
     sails as false love

blisters in a kiss?
Truth left strange and appealing
     rising as a plume

The thought revealing
from its still center
     like the rose

bared wisdom of this Stranger
in echo of the Soul . . .

On the journey taken through a tortuous road in the magnificent scenery of way to Lochinver. Leaving the track to the Ben More Assynt: 3,273 feet. Inchadamph Forest: Scottish Highlands. Used in lecture of "A Vision of Truth," 1970, in the Highlands.

The poem was written one year later in which the author felt the Questions were answered.

The Orkneys

TODAYS merge from sunset
  Into afterglows. Horizon's backcloth
Of velvet-bathed crimson:
  Her midnight sky, petalled with dawn's
White rose

TOGETHER transient hours in beauty
  Where high hilltops overflow
In birth-pang's joys
  As fledgling torn on mountain rocks
Soul rose

In search for constancy and a worthy cross.
  Friendship deepens in this vast harmony
Of silent half-light
  Where Life's past rose
Where daybreak's soul

Emerges Immortal in earthly found Heavens—
  A fantasy reborn?
Perhaps!
  The kindred spirit nature masks
Rose land

Rose sea
  JOINS longest day with shortest night
Our oneness shore
  In birthday's real awakening
Here is nature supreme
        In Flight . . .

The poem was written in 1969, a year after exile, and expresses the fullness
of poems "Night Above a Thousand Feet" and "Reality in Vision"—that
it is the essence of the true Spirit awakening and is now in 1981 (June 22)
the moment between supreme silences which hold for all time that endowed
trust and fellowship. For this reason I dedicate it to the inspiration born
of fellowship with those I love—have loved—herein contained.

February Gems

Soft lips of grass that whisper as I pass
    where frost still seals
the fronds of bracken brown in silent ground:
as sunshine tossed above stray mist and cloud
    cannot be found.
Mirrored in glass the wings of swans glaze as they pass
    perchance to catch unwary fish
where myriad eider duck, gulls with fervor seek: pluck
with cool murmuring in blue-shadowed deep harvest swish
    of waves soft that break only sound:

as blossoms snowdrop pure in virgin bed sure
    of February's Spring call
eyes raised to glacé mountaintops gilded granite rocks
Cairngorm wink in secret knowledge of their wealth untold,
    their precious stones mock
of our measured wealth when stealth of crystal light rends
    rude Heavens in twain; reflect
on smiling hills, sunburst from frost's hand that mills
and flutes in silvered flowers, in minarets white ivory
    —Towers—
    . . . the Guided Hand that wills . . .

In the Cairngorms, published in *Poetry Panorama,* 1971.

Warmth in the "secret knowledge" of a wealth untold, at peace.

White Crests of Iona

They rode the sands as mountains
  glittering green
    tossed wild
      giant waves
        tumbling fell
in a foaming white hell
        where guillemôt cries—

as a crowded mind and desires which beat
  with body craves—
    how lost to find
      as the foam whipped
        between each creek
        all emotion lies
spray-rise in an Eternity
        of motion's tidal race—

her knife-diamond wind
  thundered shout
    to whisper . . .
      as dancers toiling
        gallant and silk-white
        on float
of sable surfs
        this constant night—

Where Columba sent his Monks
  to educate:
    here from the flame
      the vice of wave
        On wave
        where guillemôt cries
          minds chorus raves
enraptured; rippled as sand-white
Healed
  as the machair starred with flowers—

Their silhouette on cliff,
  the golden shore of birds
    tossed wild—
      giant waves

tumbling
fall
on mind's horizon of green plains.
Reality in awe of granite abbey—
the touch of the
Almighty's Hand
upon man
and
granite rock
island . . .

February 1970.

A perfect peace which is found only on the island.

The Wilderness

As once, when sorrow bared my heart—
Broke every string; severed the love and drew apart:
Still in the night 'midst madrigals I pray
For cloistered image of a past to shelter lay.

As storms and tempests in their havoc cleave—
Hell's fury bent the mind does not conceive:
Blinded by torment, tossed but not afraid . . .
The fever passes, surprising, haunting ghost is laid!

The emptiness, time-honored foot on stair?
In weariness the wanting, broken dream beyond repair?
The love that shredded to destined, dreaded catacomb
Unfolds as dove's flight resurrected from the tomb:

The heart of man born fledgling to be free . . .
For as you judge so shall it meted be—
Naked the soul when still small voice combat,
The answer returns truth a kindred spirit's habitat.

First published in *Poetry Zodiac,* 1971.

As in "White Crests of Iona": "this constant night . . ." The answer as
the wave on wave reveals the Truth.

Waiting

Can love be but a day away?
  Does memory sway
Blest image of a heart's return
  When latchkey turns?

In parting: waiting interprets prayer
  Remembered there;
Ghost scenes combine secret despair
  Stills rocking chair.

Chords thorn sweet as spinnet lie—
  Notes born to die
When memory of a love still waits
  Stealing heartbreaks:

Will all the joys and whispered whys
  Where sanctuary prays
Be portals bearing shrine of time—
  Mellow wine?

Shall fate joker-howl of pack
  Call my love back?
A wheel of fortune roulette wind
  Shivers down-spine.

Be it in lifetime; balm of Spring—
  No conjuring
Faith sweet-deep her stillness calls
  Where rose petal falls—

Softer than soil in Summer rains
—He came—retain
Of lone footfall leaves no mark on sand
Yet held my hand . . .

Oban, 1970.

Published in *Poetry Zodiac*, 1971. Judged London Literary Award; highly commended by John Smith, ed., *Poetry Review*. Highly commended by *Envoi*, 1973.

In all waiting there is contemplation, sometimes remorse, anxiety, and the sorrow of inevitable fear of loss. Loss was my gain as versed in the following poem in spiritual wealth.

I Found a Loving People, Lord

I FOUND A LOVING PEOPLE, LORD
when my heart had disobeyed
I did not know which way to turn
THEY did not know how sore afraid . . .
I found in lonely people, Lord, an answer
to my prayers . . .
THEIR way of life not strange to me
spent quietly in childhood years.

I FOUND A PEACE I thought was lost
in grace of mountainside,
it stole my heart and gave straight back
YOUR wisdom, my lost pride.
I found in losing self and wealth how close
You came to me . . .
one sure step upon this rocky climb
embalms in World Brotherhood and Peace
for all Eternity . . .

The original poem first composed in Oban in 1970 when in exile.

Published in *Pilgrimage,* 1972.

First read at the Towyn Baptist Fellowship Holiday Home in 1972; sung
to music composed by a visiting minister to the fellowship by a guest tenor,
Mr. Morgan and the author, 1973. Read at Oban Cathedral by author, 1973;
Iona Abbey, 1973; B.B.C. Scotland (Poetry Programme), 1973; B.B.C.
Charlie Chester Programme, Summer, 1974. Sent as request poem to Dr.
Amado M. Yuzon for inclusion in *International Anthology on World
Brotherhood and Peace,* published in 1979. Promoting the objective of the
World Congress Peace and Poets' Movement founded by United Poets
Laureate. Published in community news and parish magazine (the Romney
Marsh Group of Churches), January, 1979.

Between the Monuments

(The stone of sound . . .)

I believe
when in such clear, dear visions these
are almost in a breathless touch: Kerrera,
Mull, between the gripping monuments
        of sound . . .

Vibrating waters flap as a gull's wing
lap on anemone, fish breathe
bask on granite-quiet stone
        of sound . . .

Could such water be cruel?
Could my heart turn to stone?
Lose breath where the emerald grass
        finds me alone?

I believe
if there's a stony sleep
then faith is my home
HERE where the silence echoes

Caves in dead leaves
        Alone . . .

Viewed from the Terrace, Oban Bay Monument. Published in *Poems of Time and Place,* 1974.

A wealth of faith.

Étive of Soft Noontide

From the Brander Pass
where the white swan kneel
in an ageless frame
'round a black, deep wheel
    of water:
                a brindled eagle soars
                from her aerie breeze
                where a red deer cries
                with her calf on snows
                in cathedral high above

wind-brushed steep bank
of shore—hill farms small:
a short call of the boat
all excitement—the POST—
Fun of cairn's gay abandon
in duet ripple of fin—
    swim of green glass waters:
                Étive's waters:

                By Loch's cool-soft sand
                gay merganser feed
                ripple the warm midstream
                as the young, gray seal
                frisk on the age-worn rock
                flecked blue-gray,

As cattle bask
on the charm of hill
where brief lies life—
between cory and bridge
from rocks and sheer ridge
valiant mountain's embrace
of her lovely
    —serene mountain waters:
                heathered as water:

                Holding pain in beauty—
                as impulse of thunder,
                where the shadowed swing
                of a white willowed sail
                carries a kittiwake, seals
                her shrill mountain cry
                    —locks the sound above her. . .

1970. The small craft goes from shore to shore delivering mail, bread, groceries, etc., to the farms and crofters: no deliveries in winter!

A wonderful experience away from civilization . . . to which I have returned many times in the next years and in 1977.

At the Calf Sales

Noblesse oblige . . .
An infringement of his rights
in the small, damp, sawdust ring
as the young, black bull bellows
from his thunderous, humerous cringe!
The hard, hot-hammer beat of the auctioneer,
monotonous rasp of a thin-timbred voice
in expectant and wasplike: "One hundred guineas, gentlemen?"
"Na'e—do I na'e hear more?" drumming
"Can y'na'e think o' Spring upon Spring . . .
and the new calves?" the young Hereford bull roared . . .
I kept quite still.
It was merriment to dare, the thrill
to own, here . . .
Bidding began again: "One hundred—one hundred and four . . ."
I sat hard on a high-tiered sawdusted bench
between a squelch of dung
and moved to the strong rhythmical equations, stench
sting of the Emporium . . .

A classic this
if one ignored beefburgers at my elbows,
multiflavored chips, odd cans of beer,
worn lineaments with the tweeds of money,
mellowed happy-fat snores from quiet farmers with sunny
smiles, shrewd in having bought and sold, now bored!
A fair drift of manure with a spiral of smoke rings
a cow's soft lament from a distant dog's barking;
the hot, cursed remorse of a loser and a solid content
in the intense, tight circle of bidders railing the ring:
heads a'scratching, elbows bent to the double sting
of finger-poised waiting—
a raised cigarette—such secretive baiting . . .

St. Bruno Flake? or was it the Condor Moment . . .
Scents of hill farm; good malt whiskey and honey . . .
good money following hard on good money!
I had lost the quick count
a spell in breath taking . . .
a'catching of crooks mellowed and horny
with the bull long since caught

31

sold at One-fifty—or was it sixty?
Mallet with farmer's sticks brisk
then a golden prance into the ring
of a small Highland calf, a pedigree—I sat a'dreaming . . .
If I had one acre, one croft, and a burn,
if I once rode a horse, could I not milk a cow?

Noblesse oblige . . .
Too old in the tooth?
Forty—fifty—fifty-six
I must have nodded my tartan tammy-topped head
for sheep in their hundreds pastured
when a resonant voice said:
        "Madam, do I then take your bid?"
Twixt the thud of the bidding and the mead I was tethered
in heather-filled meadows; furze, mid low-Highlands green,
from breeds of cattle and Exile long tarried I plead:

        "Gentlemen, forgive me, please . . .
If, when in haze of mist, rich autumnal sun
I, with white-faced Romney Marsh sheep
was totally lost in this whimsical Highland
oblivion!

        "Auctioneer, forgive me then, please.
discount my bid
this infringement of calf rights
for in three-storey-high tenement I live . . ."

Oban, 1970.

Highly recommended: *Envoi,* 1973. "A very competent poem. Original
theme, pace and drive excellent," three judges and editor J. C. M. Scott.
Published in *Horizon,* 1974. Silver Jubilee Prize Poem: *Highland Arts,*
published by Collins, 1978. C. John Taylor Awards, 1980. Exhibited at the
Studios: Easdale, 1976-1977. Book award.

Queen Elizabeth II quite often sends stock to the Oban Sales. For those
who love any kind of "sales" it is a unique experience!

When Leaves Lament

(Armistice Day by Oban Memorial, 1970)

When leaves lament
the still, gray street: leaves wingèd silent spill
from trees as ooze of blood from Sunday's loins
    leaves—
as fingered bell tolls to its close
in lilt of scarlet skeletons'
    leaves
pale toiling sun her breath-web clung
in wraith of purest air
a sea-ghost in lamp of morning
just begun:

when leaves lament
the harvest of skies wintry frown;
an arctic wind howls from fringe of fresh torment,
boughs each pulse—toll of mellow tree
where warm leaves framed
Scotland's festooned memory:
Now each pebbled foot springs the memorial
to sacred dead—
Rain floods on strength of long-armed breeze
her amber leaves . . .

When leaves lament
sweep as wet silk and choke upon the grass
to gasp
in veined red cross of love:
    leaves
lament the firmament of bagpipe sound—
the pilgrimage from sun's ripe shed
where poppy blooms again
her beau geste—

where leaves lament
in banter where tongue of fire has licked
those wounds till only geese—
cold platter of those glossy evergreens
are left . . .
    in solitary moments three

we shall remember all those
We leave
　　when leaves lament—

Read in Oban Abbey, 1971.

Received diploma for Excellence, February, 1983. In the Scottish National Poetry Competition (open), it took 7th place from 5,714 entries. Publication in the Award Book of Honour, 1983.

35

A First Matinée

When a wicked Spring wind howled
in afternoon
I cautiously half-opened
my stout mahogany front door:
to a soft Gaelic voice a brimming hat pours—
"Miss Browning?" . . . "I wasn't quite sure . . ."
"Please do come in, Mr. Smith? . . ."
He, more than a little out of breath
From a spiral to my third floor:

"There's fresh tea brewing in the pot . . .
        something *stronger*? or not?"
Now, with his back to the hearth's hot flame,
a wide singing kettle, coal and peat frame
compliment poet; author, teacher and fame!
"This . . ." said he " . . . is a very nice flat,"
looking around puffing a second cigarette,
voice soft above the windowpane in lashed-high
Rain . . .

"Yes, it is, I like it, thank you, Mr. Smith . . .
a second cup? . . . without or with?"
A malt pause of a second thought halcyon:
"I really MUST renew my London
subscription!" With cake and tea forgotten!
"A pancake, or hot buttered scone?"
"Yes, *please*"—same breath—" . . . you really *must*
        meet George MacKay Brown—
now Norman MacCaig . . ." smiled we, so thin ice broken!
"Yes," I said: "I have heard all about
Mr. MacCaig's English vows devout . . .
his Highland views" . . . laughter tinkled the teacups—
merrily mused
in the nine force gale room "rock"—
to a gentle and slow tick of the mantle clock:
"I love all the Isles, Iain, the Hebrides . . .
All your white sanded and weathered rock shores—"
A long malt pause: "*I* see scenery in white and black,"
Iain said and added: "I have recently lost my mother,
She lived with me . . .

36

YOU see it *now* in color . . .
No, I *don't* like readings in public, Stella . . . "

The manuscripts wave as water; salt to the floor,
draught as a ghost under the second door—
as smoke curled within the peat-warm room,
with the Gaelic soft and a kettle-quick hum
spins from here to Eternities driftwood shore . . .
Cigarette smoke oozed through a breasted chimney:
"I will bring you my love poems and elegies . . ."
Outside empty fish boxes skate and road-float
with the drum as Highland pipers stream—
cold-thread their way to the pier's soaked plaids . . .
Steamer bearded aft to the bay's waist-pleated seas . . .
The local gale howls—
where laughing-gull wings stinging in hail,
as inside the manuscripts lie as bread—fish-stale!

My lonely-one gull shrieks above the violent Spring storm
on the early-bulb windowbox dances, performs
in transported delight . . . frenzied as I
when Dundee cake crumbs I toss to his one greedy eye!
The room spills; as suddenly bathes, sprays with brine—
joins sun's rainbowed arc of Matinée . . . wine

Said Iain, " . . . I *was* in Harrogate, do you know it?
          Once, you know! A long time ago . . .
          For I don't often over the Border go!"

The mandate of *Pilgrimage* manuscripts
Brew
to the music from Lewis—
to the distant roar from the shore—
to the vapors of indoors—volte-face
mirror the floor . . .

Tea with Iain Crighton-Smith in Oban, 1971, when reviewing my *Pilgrimage*
MS.

Talking at Midnight

"I am too smug," he said.
"No evil has yet happened to me—
nice house, nice wife, nice kids,
nice job which I enjoy.
All my life I've been blossoming;
when will that day come 'round
when I too shall be touched
by the common spreading frost
or by the sudden wind
that brings down hearth and roof?

Have I prepared enough,
or do I find in myself
the fear that I'll be exempt
from my happy perch looking down
at those who die and drown
while I chirp here alone,
voyeur of that glory and change?"

Reign of Pastoral Silence

(As seen through the binoculars near Fort William)

RAIN on the blue-green world
a mile away
a heart-song in harp-long untold music
composed with the spoken note of wing—
flight on a quiet high flight of birds,
accompanied by a warm evening breeze
as iris movement free in amber grass, wet reeds
stir with nod of foxglove spire
their swamp command of stem wave-on-wave in bracken's lyre . . .

Reign on the blue-green world
as sunset steals the lowland pasture's bear
the pained sensitivity of quiet.
Only the blown wool coils
sheathed in breath of time-spun wires:
here sheep amble, her lambs softly graze,
here constant settings, heather roundelays!
Hills flowing range keeps permanence
with winding thread of tread-ribbon road.

Reign on the blue-green world
wind-twisted tree
you bear gently the low load
of twining honeysuckle; weeping broom's
tone foot in oak's dark shared gloom,
of pebble-truth your feet akin
and goldcrest's secret sound stirs fir within!
Slumbering brown duck, your wing in feint cloud cries
above the loch: O shadowed deep's blue lies

Marooned in rain on blue-green world
rippled in rings denote of salmon rise . . .
A mile away
a heron's flight unfurled
curls above a blue-green world
in binocular's opaque release
the tranquillity of all peace:
all light . . .

as opening of heart wide
wings close softly in tonality
of love song chord unsung—

Reigns on the blue-green world
a trembling harmony of absolute solitude
a mile away
from cloud . . . belfried cloud . . . and crowd . . .

1970.

The "untold" music of Silence with Light.

Jet's Flight in Eyes of Artisan

The wing of gull so light on air
—as dawn from jet's flight,
Dover's white cliffs of home
pulsate to château, green valley Loire . . .
eager vineyards breathe expectancy
with lowly peasantry
in homespun shawl!

A dogcart crawls in shimmering heat
of streets with green blinds drawn.
Soft speech drapes paintings in oils
from stately mirrored halls:
the aged and towering, listening trees
which border Versailles walls
where fountains through long ages play

and cascade as Paris in the Spring—
with her new loves who cling by Seine
to sing in rhapsody by night . . .
"Can-Can" to charm the lazy eye
bare ballêt scenes . . . her dreams!
Frail almond trees
as orange lantern's poise

with lemon, frame in Palma's carriage way
O quiet February day—
On wing of calm
and deep seas toil of net
where laundries in the bay hang brilliant
as "La Paloma" aired on decks:
Sound positive of castanets

in flamenco swirl of skirt brilliance
—as dawn from jet's flight
in fold of silken fans—
in grottoes, romantic caves
with champagne laced air of mountains!
Children who toil on endless sand—
Aged jewelled eyes of Artisan

—On wings of sound—

the scenes and dreams realized—
transparent in bright cushioned light
as birth of day painting her way
through ribboned folds of night!
Yes! Moonlight spills
and drowns in sunshed of quiet hills
and spirits the gull white . . .

To the charm of flight: On Wings of Sound; from Dover—Paris—
Versailles—Spain—back over the Pyrenees—Dover—Heathrow.

At Duntrune Castle

A Benediction

September rains combine, divine each clear candled
hallowed thought; transept wind-beaten stares
in falling benevolence, share

of each rod of missile rain
a sigh to an all-leaden sky!
A prism of washed, pensive summer mourns past flares

in scorch hidden, drenched stone driven
beaten cruelty of heavy rains!
Low of drowned beasts power above

where a mountain pool of crystal cries
waxed flowers overlaid
to surround her lily purity of face

in innocence, a grave castle
stands in shore-white lied path of loneliness.
Her elegy of lapped waterfalls

tunnels made merrily volatile
in motley of a simple vesper
her singing Saviour's grace . . .

Appreciation from Col. George Malcolm 29:3:72—" . . . here is the beauty
and feeling of the West Highlands, the instinctive effect of our lovely sur-
roundings upon someone other than oneself; it is truly appreciated—thank
you." (Now deceased, letter from Lady Malcolm 30:9:77.) Published in
Pilgrimage, 1972.

At the time of writing, I was visiting the castle in view of the tenancy of
the nearby cottage—and still staying in Oban with my cousin.

Breach Birth

(A crossing of the Minch *to Barra, January, Force 9 Gale)*

As her waters' break—
  and seas of water boil
—Rush—boiling over
  brimming lids curled, fringed
Awaiting birth   The surge—
—Push—   —Pain—
Retreat of every leaping wave
awaiting gain—
A toiling ship creaks—groans
as sweet suck as mouth upon the lips.
Deeps swallow unfathomed feet
as she cascades
—Rises—trembling
shuddering in the Almighty grip

Motion of wholesome woman with her babe . . .
The torn sea rips to her broad belly—wide—
cruelly coughs ships spuming, wretching sides . . .

The wind sings
  as triumphant mother
  with her newly born child!
  Delicious screaming cry above
  in rocked cradles . . .
  blankets of missile rains . . .

Thundering the searing pain waves
—aching to calmer waters
  drenched the swept deck stabilizes . . .

Remains where the afterbirth of storm
bleeds with her hidden sighs
quelled upon the reefs
and prized quayside:

stitched vibrant blacks
  shine folded   needle-wet
  —a quiet silver
  cotton-white with amber spreads

Sands' ever changing shawl
with parent-proud wind
in driven bonnets of thickly drawn mist
on a rock of moonlit rain . . .

Published in *Pilgrimage,* 1972. Published in *Times* and *Post,* 29:7:76. Highly commended by June Chisholm. Highly commended by John Smith (Prize Poems: 1971, London). Highly commended by editor, *Poetry Review.* Published by Tagore Institute of Creative Writing in *The Album of International Poets,* 1981.

This and the following four poems are rich in the experience of the warmth and friendliness of the Scottish people in all adversity of the Hebridean Isles in mid winter.

"D'y'ken the Gaelic Soft Skimmed As Cream?"

The soft Gaelic voice
soft skimmed as cream
shares the dark dress of old women
through curried and flurried whispers of snow:
Ship's cargo
unloads on a milk-white jetty
in night as wild as the clawing cats
with people as warm as their cottage lights

in helter-skelter of wind low
as their hushed Gaelic voice
hunched awaiting the ship!
Minister awaiting the burial boat—
the pilot to guide
of a girl only seven;
her casket, floating the wave
where cancer had laid her ugliness . . .

Grave, where almost in world untouched
croon the warm Gaelic voices
their true welcome awaiting
in whiskey heartwarming
share of storm unrelenting!
This siren-she wind shrieking . . . *never* abating?
where the lightship safely winks . . . and the keepers
week's waiting . . .

Sea—where Barra Island waits, waits for cargo
always—WAITING—
The sheltering sheep
turn as human's back to the wind in the lee of front doors . . .
then move in the half-light as strangers
who lived there before?
Dawn with her shepherdess crook whistles
her flocks from hawk's high shelves of the moors!

As a thin Gaelic smile
twists this corkscrew road—
the car following tails of the sheepdogs . . .
Did this cow frisk as she "jumped over the moon?"
Were the proud, stout and ambling

Ancients cloaked, muttering?
Four sheltering hens
cackle and fight
for shelter "windowsill rights"
so the wind cuts her corners, lashes the hail:

Night telegraph wires buzz with a crisp gossip tale
then teacup foretell fortune of folk
who y'ken; d'y'ken—
this soft Gaelic voice
bare-sweet note of mountain,
dark as shore blue-bottle . . . washed . . . sand-deep and ocean?

Barra, 1971.

Sand-White Shore at Northlay, Castlebay, Barra

On powdered white sand
pound great shining sheets of glowing jade
tumbling down blanched to pillowed scattered foam
of feather white:

Duet in a steel shrieking wind
her knife edge cutting raw my heart, bare stone
weeps with shelved crystal snow
dance of gnomes in a no-man's land
on spinning hard white sands:

This barren land of rock
sugar gleaming running granite rock
in four treeless land grins wide
a lip-pink raw-gum gape her torn-apple
crab-mouthed dawn!

Her fanged teeth of winter's gale
in nine force chews the tight bleeding strata
of skinned skyline!
A STATUE I present, no poem—
her carved and naked virgin-sweet
        all barren . . .

January, 1971, written at the home of Compton McKenzie where he wrote "Whiskey Galore" overlooking the shore from "Suidhiachan." Published in *Envoi*. " . . . presents a vivid picture of this outer Hebridean Island," E. G. Pickthall, 1977. Chosen for poem for Hertfordshire *Ipse*, 1978, by Robin Gregory (who then retired). Published in *Poetry International*. Published in *New Hope* magazine, Spring, 1982.

A January Muse on Barra

SING to the music in this wind . . .
the baton of a song without an end
how wealth of Creation beats within each

choked and dried blade of grass:
summer seed stirred, sought by sour sun
sand-sedge root deep in encroaching sands

and roots in sand were said to never last?
Here it still rides the crest of dune
waves its salt-wind spike to Heaven

and where the drift hills deeper still
I play in beaten time ultramarine—
the grass my hand, my feet the sand

and I am caught in million years
where sand accumulates new bristles rise . . .
Moonlight to carry all my ferried nights
            in stars . . .

The equal loneliness of poem "In Guadeloupe I Pick a Flower."

Ormistons

Cottage of Memory

Alone: where the cool water smiles
all earth and heaven beguiles
      this summer's day:

where are the shadowed sighs?
Eventide breakers lie soft on the shore
      of yesterday!

Dimmed by the leaf-green light my shadow spills
into the evening wind
      tamed by blind hills

Wisdom of sea and song
of the thrush: no man an island is
      where there is love.

Sea—where the bluebell drops into a haze
of twilight-blue sleep—
      universe of self

Sense and sound, pulse round the wind—
wise to this languid grace
      aroma pure summer wing:

Bowing to delight time a lone spider spins
caught by sun's fingered light
      in crazy, festooned

Wave of silver companioned night—
a-strengthen in dusk, heart's flight
      from wandering!

Into the solemn shade of arch rustic—
tempered gray stones,
      fragrance of woodsmoke

Uncharted isle beat of night
a musical soul in her musing: flight—
      —fall silent and quiet—

Swift when watersmeet, internal storms
poison as ivy clings to honeysuckles'
    pure vine:
O may these thick walls speak
and as rime clings to bark
    may the stains of grim time
    Die—with the past—

Written at the cottage adjacent to Duntrune Castle on the Poltalloch Estate.
A view from the window of the cottage of the loch was painted in water
color by the author. In the adjacent field a picture in oils of horse and foal
which was born when in residence.

Published in *Panorama*, 1971. *Pilgrimage and Other Poems* was commenced
here, also the Children's Verses of *The Adventures of Hoodie the Crow,*
true story with illustrations.

Ormistons

An April Sea Symphony

(The return of the Grey Lag Geese, North West Scotland)

Where a wild harmonica of skies—
   notes as a violin, ride a high
goose-gaggled play
    sleek-grey above a caravan
in a blue harpsichord of migrant duck—
   netted each their croak—beak
—striking beak of honey chord—

Swift as a wing of a late sand-martin,
   brittle as turned reeds of played sand
where the grey lag's overture
    gather to a rhythmed pipe band:

I race—how breathless
         stand
"Under the shadow
     of Thy wings
       will I rejoice"
Where the breeze gallops
steeps high and horns wide:
    funnels in a sweeping chase—
on a bold seaweed red strand!
    An opaque laugh, eerie pound
of two bone-dry, storm-lost leaves
    where the sprayed stones rattle in sound!

Wintered-grasp of a hawk turns prey within
         reach
of each taunting and rigid grave found:

Where the grey lags their octave slim-beat,
   beaked on shimmering dwarfed rivers in sand!
Pure keyed harmonium—string breeze
   harness April to her chariot seas
in a salt-winged caress on goblin-gloved waves:
   under the shadow
      thin finger-soft rain
       flying—milking
       —white crests

Mark of the island's peace in her gale
nine force dress—and a grey lag seas' symphony
    borrows her evening's furrow,
where finale is her good earth to rest . . .

"Under the shadow of Thy wings I will rejoice" (Psalm 63).

Highly commended by Norman Hidden, *New Poetry*. One of three poems accepted by the Silver Jubilee Highland Arts on exhibition at Seil Island Studios, 1977. Received the Poem Book Award.

The poem in preparation when Prince Philip was staying at Duntrune Castle.

Sails in the Thirsting Wind

Sails in the thirsting wind
Anchors free of the hook and coiling sands
Mast high and fancy free
As birds her pearl flood of encircling hands:

Fish-white shoal-hunt in a rainbow's end—
Rain in the wind—grin
Grind of harsh sea on a double-bowed boat,
Rush of wave—fall of a whale's fin:

Mill of the wind; thrash in wind of dark
Of a tongued, mantled reel—
Where stars caught as fish in a rain of God's lips,
Blue lightning's flame as deep steals

Our fish! Wild water leaps when God held all cloud
—Reflects in moonshine's net:
Whales crimson in flood, fire of mackerel skies!
Soft silver lie in gut harpoon-met

Of mast points fleshed high:
Sails in the thirsting wind
Where Galilee rose in a calm glow of dawn's virgin eye!
Loaves baking in a diamond bed
With
A cruel kind of wisdom harvested.

Whaling in the North Sea, 1970.

To be asked to partake in this whirlwind of physical and mental exhaustion
is the wisdom of the sea . . .

The Natural Flower of Friendship
for One Week Was Mine

For one week was mine:
Her Mull-breath of earth so worldly wise
Her ocean surround of rising suns
Her old visions in the new belong:

In a belfried cloud dance of endurance
Her built-in white sea mists
Tether her geese with swan's feathered scenes

Painting her waters cream in bays—
Her whispers across toned rippling sand
In winter-strong wind speaks of pageant dreams

Here solemn raised, sincere yet gossamer sad!
Cool as Mull's low voice where cruel waters
Bare the penetrating garden of her mind:

Ben More strikes at living sky
Buries the flushed face of moon—
Pierces the constant reign of sun,

Her island kiss on dews; as stars bathe in unknown
Seas of beauty, leaving a sparkling smile
On Tobermory tiptoed in a naked dawn!

Tomorrow's laughter spills from lips
Burning in her ice-blue snow clasp
As deep's hand with yesterday's warm fish.

May I keep a latchkey to this island's frondose—
Her Mull-breath and smile of worldly wise,
Her visions new to me belong—
A thank you for one week was mine . . .

Written and read at the "Little Mull Theatre," 1971. "Very descriptive with
good and satisfying lines," J. C. Meredith-Scott, editor, *Envoi*, 1978.

A "softer" isle's kiss of Mull-breath . . .

The Search

When I called
and the echoes wound 'round like wool
blows in the wind as the cotton sedge—
dances above the thick coniferous woods—
where I took to the path high on the heath
and saw the old nests of snow bunting and pheasant.

When I called
and the echoes dropped like lead—
dropped on the ground where mother Hoodie hurt her leg,
I found more deserted, much used nests
in low trees; in crags, of kestrels and buzzards
lined with bracken and dried withered grasses . . .

When I called
and remembered the clutch of blue eggs,
the speckled and lovely one of red,
kestrels and peregrines had feathered the trail,
nests with sticks on a grassy ledge,
frosty leaves tucked in a rabbit burrow.

When I called
I knew Hoodie wouldn't be on the cool loch shore
I knew he wouldn't be with the carrion crows
but where in the world was Hoodie by now?
So tired I sat by an old peregrine's nest
Still soft with sedge, wool and perched on sticks . . .

When I called
stroking the lined hair; long grass, the soft
wood rush, I sat and listened hard and long
for a croak or a scream, a rustle on stone—
a flutter of wings now Hoodie was almost grown:

"HOODIE . . . " I cried, picking the yellow coltsfoot stems
sheltering low with me from the west wind . . .

"The Search," poem from *The Adventures of Hoodie the Crow,* book pub-
lished in 1981. Passed Kent Board of Education for Schools. Taken for use
in exhibitions with the National Book League, Scotland Tour, 1982. Given
in full reading with the Poetry Affiliation Meeting of the Town's Women's
Guilds at the Worthing Library in September, 1981. With full illustration
by Reverend Roland Portchmouth. A survival story in verse. Verse above
published in *Observer,* 1973.

Review from Robert Armstrong: " . . . exciting work from a new writer
with a poetic understanding of Nature, a rewarding book . . . "

Comprehensive review of the book was given by Dr. Allison Johnn-St.
Johnn, Ph.D., in May, 1981. "Hoodie . . . a delightful, captivating and
lovable creature is presented by the gifted poet-author Stella Browning in
her beautiful and inimitable verse . . ."

To Avril, the Weaver of Tweed
At Ardfern: the mainland and the shore

Let's leave the loom—and climb the stile?
    into the Wing-of-Sounds broad land of peat—
stirs fir, with her slim-on-rough foothold!

We, on our proud round whistle wiry dog
    seeking the soaked night sheep for market!
Bends arrowed arch of catkin, willow—

In steel, frightened and glowing eye of ewe,
    from peeping yellowed eyes of gorse
now stumbling slakes in early dew,

Streaks stalking mountain cat off-course—
We, in dry byre milking times' frolic find
Friendship and true round Highland hills wide:

In that bleak hour before the dawn that strove
    to hold back the dark of night—
As lover conscious only of the will

That drives black shadows to unwanted light—
    let's *hold the sound* of wings—hooded—
hidden, in cloak of Highland's might . . .

To Stella, the Lover of Shore

Sand, Stella—only!
    primeral rock split, blasted, shattered
    swept by whirlwinds—
        crashed, pounded, scattered:
        drowned by dark seas
        dragged by ocean flows

           to my wanderer on the beach
           just a million grains
             beneath
               her toes . . .

Poems exchanged in fun with Avril Dunn, George Orwell's sister, when the author stayed at "Gartcharron," Ardfern, Argyllshire, 1971. Copyright obtained (first publication).

61

Roast Beef and Yorkshire

At Ormistons

I had lunched at Gartcharron many times
Menu-de-resistance "Cow Pie" with wines:
Avril's "Cow Pie" was in circumference two feet!
Commanding table vegetables en-route:
creamed carrots, leeks endowed with a snow-white sauce,
potatoes "jackets on" await a second course . . .
with whiskey flowing as water on the Ardfern banks—

join Sunday's ripple on the shore of estate Poltalloch
where the turmoil of the week together we forgot . . .
Lunchtime arrives as Avril swished the drive
in battered shooting-brake: " . . . Bill, won't be long, I've
come posthaste about the new Hereford bull—
the young one you sat astride, Stella, in his stall!
Remember? . . . the docile creature *wouldn't* eat?

"stood all silent, strong in perfect young beef?
Well! this morning he is *ravenous*—
companions of night—nine ladies in an overnight seduce!
He's sound in the hay now sleeping ounces off!
I guess this five hundred pound bank loan we scoff?
He's worth his wild oat this morning graced in byre . . .
Let's celebrate this Michaelmas calf sire!"

" . . . sorry I'm late . . . " Bill; red faced, leg-pad on ground,
"I hadn't time to change my leg—you've heard?"
He stumped happily around the gray rock-slab floor,
his pad still adhered to cow-pad with mixed straw!
One good foot cowed in weekday leather:
"Forgive me," he said . . . "when dining out from Highland
weather—
I like to have time to change "the set" two brogues
          —tweed's measure . . ."

His face rain; wind tanned, pinched with sudden pain . . .
I passed the twinkling glass of Scotch neat again:
I said: "Have you not had sufficient for one day of—*Beef?* "

"Oh no! without a doubt he's a courageous fellow
   in the raw! Enough? Sunday's pleasure for me is Yorkshire—
            potato
roast—all in the tin around the Highland beef rare . . .
Nil Desperandum, Stella, ALL is certainty—*Beware!* "

Bill Dunn lost his leg while serving with the Argyll and Sutherland
Highlanders, World War II. He married Avril Orwell, sister of George, who
nursed both men back to health. She was with him when writing "Animal
Farm" on the Isle of Jura.

The Red Admiral

by LOCH ÉTIVE, in memory of my father, Beecher Daniel

I must have been born at sunrise
    taken first breath on the shore?
Laughed where the sun knit in furrows
    the layette of summer I wore?

I must have been born in a different age
    where lochs wed in green vivid mirrors
as a stage for combed tears . . .
    a magical mist's dance on a high ridge of moors
engaging dappled crisp sunshine
    in blue-coupled droplets of laughter:

I must have been born yet to be free
    as the womb cradled the egg to my destiny?
Now Autumn strips, purses her red-rough lips
    dew beads between late pink blackberry blossoms.

You fade from the loch's face, Father,
    in boughs crippled and green . . .
greener than apples hung shining, repeating
    all greens in droplets of moths
caught in delicate webs:
    LISTEN—in bracken

where a beaded dragonfly pleads
    on its cross of blackthorn:
the throttle of thrush wearing solitary wing;
    glazed eye of a rabbit wretched in brambles,

blind mole on her stair—
    quick sigh of a pheasant with vegetable atoms,
vermin at prey with a lamb's skeleton
    all trapped in a sundance,
a sun-tumble in basket of seed-ripened blackberries—
    shall we always be late, Father?

We, who roamed early as hedgerows?
    Early as marshes? As green-fallen apples?

Lost now in a low-sucking foam of evergreen branches . . .
My birth was not with a silver spoon—

Not with the gloss, gypsy sheen of the berried bowers!
Yet I turn from this blood; torn flesh, blackthorn
turn from all greens to wild pink of late flower
to destroy now the net, exile while I am still wise . . .
Free YOU, Father, your free atheist soul
You, pinioned fragile in burial flame

Stronger in death in your shimmering web:
this droplet wing
of my dear late-painted
Red Admiral

My father: *Victorian* who did not think his daughter should be a *writer* (in those days not heard of).

One of three poems accepted by the Silver Jubilee Highland Arts: on exhibition at Seil Island Studios. 1977 Book Award. Highly recommended by Robert Armstrong, 25:2:76: " . . . the essential attributes of all good poetry are here, exciting work, very fresh." Published in the *Runnymede Association of the Arts* magazine, Autumn, 1982. Also to be published with "Singing Pens," *Anthology, U.S.A.,* 1983.

Bouquêt in Glendaruel

Wild sweeping green-gray grasses
pulsed by strong listening winds
where rapids silk-wild find
my mind caressed when flowing
seeps for forget-me-not spray blowing
in dew's climb, rival of skies blue
of high July!
Cloud pure; pale, waxen breath . . .
as blithe sigh of companion-violet
in perfumed cry:

pulsed by strong listening winds
in finger white limb of May's showering!
A rosebud guest jade springs
to stem of stream—bed of crystal remembering:
Flowers picked when tender child . . .
mind heather-running mixes bouquêt wild—
white marguerites—
gold buttercups encircle daisy crowds . . .
Such petal clamor comprehends with life's
strange hedgerow happenings, of cliff's

memoried bower so clearly driven past
as orchis wild how vivid lasts
through idle blue, low cushion moss
in wild-sweeping green-gray grass!
no note of discord steals bouquêt
as upon swift light fountain bracken's brae
here rapids silk-wild find
blue summer's late and laze lustred world
the loom of sound spun flowers wild
—sleep—sleep tender as child . . .

Award poem, Scotland, 1976. *Envoi:* "So many flashes of beauty and style that I must keep reading it, I like the tenderness of the closing lines—its clever verse," Ellen E. H. Collins—passed: K.G./J.C.M. Scott/Gray/1977. Published in 1976 and 1977. A "best poem" choice. Published in Sunday *Durango Herald* in "Spotlight," chosen by Dr. John Tapia, Dept. of Foreign Languages, Fort Lewis College, Durango, Colorado, 1980.

Alone but not lonely . . .

Tomorrow

I sought the world . . .
"Who seeketh" . . . Yet shall find?
Would it be he that tarrieth not
or in the pastures of the quiet mind?

Time stands not still
She beckons—Who will follow?
Into unknown—the chasms, wingèd haunts
of open space with speed and grace of swallow?

As moonbeams dance
Galleons on the waves into uncharted waters—
Sped by the moon a lantern in the sky!
Sailset—the helmsman guided: yet whose hands
        may never falter?

Fallow the thought
Incentive find in querulous, tortured mind:
For passage of time she conquers
        reflections of our sorrow
in joys shared! Love dies? the infinite
               Tomorrow!

Heart ruleth head
If love now makes us blind?
Counts not the years—Despiseth all that scorn—
"Seek ye again" the Prophet said:
          " . . . for ye *shall* find."

Published in *Poetry Zodiac,* 1971.

Suicide Beside the Loch

You may ask me how she looked?
She lay as transparent dried
silken-white death, tall as pampas grass—
in a heart's full throated cry, her hollowed
eyes darkening cemeteries of glass:

In quiet guise, mascaràs
cool dream of apricot! Pallor reigns
in blue veins—strands of ochre hairs
once driven—brilliant warm as sand
now thatch visited by hawk?

Questions arise when I identified—
visions returned; beckoned again,
how could I not feel deep remorse?
Servile pain, hot before my eyes closed in—
severed the shadow of her cross . . .

Deep pooling sleep oblivion—
from glory drowns her human voice:
for she who had loved vast audience—
From dying now hear her poignant cry,
from salt-wave, sorrow-bitten dust

Now eddies white-smiled lie . . .
Siren—she who sung with no equal lust
but the night-jar of a wild wind sky:
Too late—this anguish to identify
from vision now this earthly songbird
            lost . . .

Oban, 1971. Published in *Envoi,* 1976.
"Striking"—Best Poem choice, P. M./ Lee/ and J. C. M. Scott, ed.

The anguish to identify a friend and soloist superb.

A Tone Poem

The Confetti of Shore-Wedded Skies in the Shetland Isles

—Autumnal rays divide—
Subside as auburn plays to rapt amethyst!
Violet draped with Heaven's turquoise—
surprised azure smiles in a billowed cloudrise!
Cream attunes as yellow bird-bills
where amber torn calls from belfried hills!
Warm pink from golden eagle edge
in slumbering rock agate steals her bed.

Quick-steel appeals to wedded Eve
from risen firm-white breasts—
cloud-molded phantom lips—
where mauve whispered, steeples into night
her candled thigh in black's woven robe—
a secret spiral-hide where white moonrise . . .
From drift of "borrowed raiment" veils
this new crescent light: the current scale of fish—

O! pale mourns the trek of Autumn-guest-dawn—
O! sunrise preens her pillow frail, her married lines
await sea's modest call of memories' lawn, apple-greens!
When emerald turns the midnight foam
from solemn black into grays—
here bleak of day tossed, trapped in mackerel steps
as daybreak wakes in lightning's flesh—
envelopes thunder roar—
Shore revelry of missile rain
finger-hard on the shoulder sand-gold ingrain

Confetti of the Isles
Rich amber sings of wedding rings, yoke-smiling
SEASHORE
  SEASHORE
    Seashore
      shore
        ore
          e

The second tone poem written, the first published. *Pilgrimage* title: "Swan Fashions: A Brief Encounter."

Both poems inspired by Northern Scotland.

An October West Highland Morning

Six-Thirty at Loch Awe

Where rowan boughs her Highland head
  Red-berries quiet in the fern
Thick mist scurries through wet bracken
  Tangles corries, combs in falls.
Crags grow gray mist their thick, long beards
  Sun-laughing go across Loch Awe
And rowan boughs her head in thorn . . .

In muted greens far hillside sleeps
  From blue-green deeps half-trims the wick
In wax flamboyant burn of flame
  Like candle turns in mountain creek
Pure amber glow brown leaf of oak
  In amble of soaked ghostly sheep
Dog rakes a pasture's symmetry
  Of Highland herd and brimming burn
And rowan boughs her head in thorn . . .

Where rowan boughs her Highland head
  In mountain whistles pulse of throat
Like Adam's apple risen gold
  Throttle of blackbird guest of worm,
The seeking hawk sears crown of morn
  In October's dank, plush-streamed grass
Clouds buried froth in greener glass.
  High heather tears a gilded shoe
And rowan berried boughs in Awe . . .

1971. Best Poem choice, *Envoi*, 1976. Published and recommended by J. C. Meredith-Scott, editor. "An arresting poem with a very individual and close-knit use of words," B. N. S., *Envoi*, 1977.

Fait Accompli

Will he come
Will he move between the rowan branches
Where the mind in vacuum dances
        in green song?

Will he stay
Will he weave into the fragrant hours
Happiness and lightning magic play
        Upon noonday?

Will he move
Will he count the changing hours
Till morning; can he prove,
        can he repay?

Will he weave
Will he remember; part the fear
From fires cold embers, leave
        the grave?

Will he count
Will he forgive; so softly grieve
For countless echoes from a height
        where love has strayed?

Will he remember
Will he never forgive and pass forever
Across the rivers of my heart
        with hollow pain?

May I always
(Yes, forever) count the cost . . .
But not in vain, may I walk
The silver maze in sunshine
        after rain . . .

Published in *Pilgrimage,* 1972. Chosen for anthology by John Smith, an editor of *Poetry Review,* London Poetry Society.

To "count the cost" . . . again in memory . . .

Paranoia

HOW DARK YOUR EYES
  how strangely change
    from watercolors' blue
      into each channelled depth
        of rage, my torment to complete
      this wish for you?

HOW DARK YOUR EYES
  yet panic not? I, afraid
  of your hold on me?
    This vicelike grip
      where I become your strong
      internal rage
        consumer of strange words

allowed to slip triumphant
  from your panting tongue!
  When paranoia rampant
    as in retrospect
      with hell's unnatural pressures

forced upon my lips!
  Released from steeple-bell ringing—
  controls this paralysis
    Your fingertips?
      How surprised you will be—

HOW DARK YOUR EYES
  remembering not the vague
  blue-sear of neck?
    The fatality of infidel
      and chill-hear rustle only
      in your loved trees lonely . . .

You cannot ask forgiveness
  without conscience and true
    when I only know
      in your fire-burns maddening
      sickness, swollen eye
      all embers glow:

HOW DARK YOUR EYES
and smolder then impromptu
tracing your delicate, long
strong fingers
in their white-interlace
relentless as the strong
vice of snows . . .

Published in *Envoi,* October, 1976. "A valiant poem on a most difficult subject," Gray.

Marriage of Fleet with Storm at Sea

*On a bleak morning's return of the fishing fleet off Stornaway,
1970*

Where violence breaks with storm at sea . . .
  bow-breaks in spumed violet wave
turning as giant-flamed cathedral spire's fuseé
  —rise with thunder roll above sea grave:

Springlike as an ocean's virgin kiss, swells
  her body-proud, bashful as a new bride!
Her white-foamed barren body falls
  upon deep's searock, midnight hard they ride . . .

Skies mullioned window fired in mooncry;
  quarter-veiled as in birth's face,
swift as font waters pour: a babe's speechless sigh
  in rock of a limbless tidal race:

When lightning strikes upon the shore
  this Herculean fleet from grim labor rests—
proud surge of "lion to lamb" where burn rains pour
  —sand-beat as giant bared with morning breast:

In a gulled-cold count of the fishing fleet
  in surrounding strand of seaweed-red sleep
these valiant men! Where fish silver-nodding on sheet
  of emerald the marriage speaks—
      of violent storm at sea
        with the men who
          go down
            to the
              deep . . .

The last experience before moving to my flat in Oban from the cottage.

Old Men Within Blue Grass

From the local "Working Men's Club" night
  music thunders on the vibrant air
for shift where steep the forgotten coal tips:
  black Alps great pulse from womb
                 to tomb

Throbbing black echoes in endless door-to-door streets
  frame stooping men; torn limb and lung
    rattle and cry in pain
where years of hurt from coalmine dirt
    their fear in eyes remain

Rattling in the profound silence . . .
  in underground tomb lies lust; their joy in life,
a sorrow that shields in grotesque shape
  as moon in a thick morning mist:
    the living hive of white-faced
               Women

with shopping basket; shawl, head scarf covering curlers—
  time for the fish and chips,
    time for his local brew
      in smoke-tired skies
        sun-drowned in smile

within a flood of blood red—song thrush of lilacs
              Lavender:
Seeking his own passion after truth
           sings to the blind
           sings to the cold
the silent men within blue grass . . .

A mining village near Barnsley, 1969. The scene as viewed at that time and place by author.

Published in *Envoi*, 1977. A best poem choice: "Beautiful poem," Editorial panel: Wesley, Lee, Meredith-Scott. "Will find a place in one of our magazines, lovely descriptive poem," Robin Gregory, *Poetry International*, 1977. Further review of poem 1978 by panel: "An absorbing poem to be read and reread with the benefit of additional insight into the theme with each contact. The poetry is beautiful and original," November, 1978. Also published by Tagore Institute of Creative Writing in their magazine, *Ocarina*, July, 1982. The author the European editor of the magazine.

From Minaret

(To Bunny)

From a soft trespass of wave
Where a foot's crushed implant in sand,
as a heart when the soul understands.
    On a high musical tread
as a glaze of a soft-singing breeze
       where a river tolls to the sea
       gathers her threads . . .

As a bell in an ocean of tides
       your love and mine . . .
As a reflection mullioned windows in time
dusks seaward hill grows — leaps
       pleads — unwinds
       Siphons in flood as a siren's sweet scream
       the impossible dream —

The above poem in reference to poems pages 119-126. Published in *Pilgrimage* 1972. Chosen by John Smith, editor *Poetry Review*, from selection, 1970.

Mull of Kintyre

1970

Riding through clouds
Leaden the sky—no murmuring sounds
As Heaven breaks in dawning peach-blossom edged
On winged morning rests:

Mull of Kintyre
Widens her plain; broad hills, her noble spires
As bird's eye seen, strands fold in nature's plaits of green
To crown as Queen!

On thick matted backs
Clawed by black crow seeking the warmth it lacks
Of ewe's sodden fleece in January's rains,
Torn in her pains.

Wends tractor with hay
To herds, patient "ladies in waiting" pray
As silent they muzzle to steal each away
From sombre gray day.

The Coast Road to Campbeltown . . .

Wild horses ride
Water's green bosom swells in pride becoming tides
Of streaming frosted juggler's patterns played
On white-sanded bay:

Salt spray o'er rocks
King heron firm of foot so coldly mocks
The cadenced flying manes of spumier brine
Where granite fingers shine,

Seaweed still cloys
Round jetsam, flotsam ghosts of children's toys
Shipwrecks of transient suns trade winds pursuing finds:
Only the tranquil mind

79

Of crystal sea-green
Fast ropes caught in channels to turn waves deep cream
Cascades translucent, falls swollen to stream

Deepening my dream!

London Literary Award, 1971. Judged by poet and author John Smith, editor, *Poetry Review*. London Poetry Society. Published in *Pilgrimage,* 1972. Published in Scottish magazines and read on the Islands. Further acclaimed 1976 and reviewed by Harold Mayes, editor *Times* and *Post,* July: " . . . and who has been to the tip of the Kintyre peninsular stretching its long finger round the Firth of Clyde who would *not* appreciate . . . " the above! Given in readings Oban High and Southlands Schools, 1974.

I Was a Spy

"You're not allowed up there," he said.
Smart uniform in dark blue serge
Of Cavalry's United States,
His companion sheathed in gorgeous plumage red
Where weather-beaten Indians lie
And chant the war cries
For the dead!

The bugle sounds remuster
"Where is the troop?" I said,
"Can't you see, ma'am, we're all that's left.
The company has fled?"

The mounties grinned from ear to ear
"We'll escort you back to barracks,
Have no fear . . . "

A SPY was all they needed
To complete the victorious fray
        Why spoil their fun
When bath-time's just an hour away?
The war cries hush to lullabies
With roll call read
The war paint, Indians and whole platoon alive
Are safe in bed!

An award poem. Published in *Envoi*, 1972. Remarks: " . . . has universality and original approach, all good through especially ending," R. W. Wesley, Lewis-Smith, editor J. C. Meredith-Scott. Published in *Pilgrimage* 1972. Published in *Horizon* magazine, 1974. Popular in readings.

Resulted from being nursemaid for a day!

The Bark Between

Whippendell Woods, Watford

I saw her once . . . harsh winter cloak
   shrugs her shoulders, draws a frown
stout frame lean to brown, rigors
   of winter claim her silence, name a tomb . . .
as canine friends chase snow to tail
—raise, pause in merriment their bark
caught rigid as the silent park:

a pilgrim in white reverie
   I saw her wear cool bluebell gown
silver birch a soft-shoe dancing,
   yews shelter safe from April's tears,
sweet budded may, elf celandine,
   still bush bereft of thoughts of rest,
songbirds who break quick world in twain . .
   nest, hover onto twig, wind their refrain

to pilgrim in blue reverie
   I saw her last midsummer dress
in common place, sash creased in rest,
   her face wears breath of England's breeze
leaf-smile to web, rough wave of keys,
   her nature pure as classic charms
spin oak, gray ash, broad walk of elms,
   a hazel slips to armed thorned-berry

a pilgrim in green reverie
   I shall see her wear this autumn best
she'll dress again in height of fashion
   where the shadows tread her russet dress
will I feel strange, a shabby guest?

82

An ecstasy of fluttering wings
blushed hurrying wind whips treetops free,
    swift squirrel sweeps a leaf along, a glimpse
of sky 'neath swifts bend to the willow

    when reverie keeps for a while . . .

Published in *Pilgrimage*, 1978.

It was from this memory of the woods that the children's verses were
"seeded" and written over a period of three years when in exile in Oban.
Title, *Butter in the Buttercups,* Parts 1 and 2; part 3, a winter sequence,
finished at Elstree.

83

"You Are Walking in My Shadow"

Whippendell Woods

"You are walking in my shadow, Nanny . . ."
  So softly said her fair head turned toward mine
between each towering fir, elms laced
with sparkling April sunshine!

  Low willows dance with murmuring spring
as gypsies tangle:
  Where YOU once turned your head from me
and cried:

  As a broken woodpecker's note
drum beats—harshly strums
  his deep throat breaks—

Where so softly sing now the young . . .

"Nanny, why is your shadow longer now than mine?"
Are puddles darker, reflections deeper
  than our woods in sunshine?

Why, in retrospect these sentinels were black
  in cool-dripping English rain—
    and now? Pooling skeletons of old almanac

Holding those stronger secrets from me
  when You cried!

I know within these shadows stirred are fir cones
  spilt, lapping a new carpet in the sun,
    as new seeds spin hungrily—

happily sown
      running past me;
        cheeks, wider eyes glowing:

"Isn't your shadow shorter now than mine?"
    Sing softly, Julie,   •
      between our deep green pines . . .

In retrospect to J.
From Oban; written on a return to Watford where I had lived for over a
period of twenty years after first leaving New Romney after World War II.

85

A *Poem from* Butter in the Buttercups

Poem from the Children's Verses—
story told of Whippendell Woods

"Nanny . . ." hurriedly
"Do you think the Woodcutter
Left our Washing-machine?" laughs Julie
   Racing, tumbling down the steep, mossy hill
"YES—YES" and Stuart's picnic basket spills—

Now picnic spreads on oaken table
   Napkins spinning in the breeze,
Rabbits peeping from strange burrows
   Squirrels racing the large plane trees,
Was this then a miracle

Or would we all waken on a pinnacle
   Of wilder forest dreams?
Tiny BUTTERCUPS cute fairy rings
   Folding flowers of yellow globe
Yes, BUTTER IN THE BUTTERCUPS is sown

Forget-me-nots spread far their seeds
   Scales above softly hooded greens,
As Julia dancing where the milkwort,
   Stuart where violet's green of heart is caught,
Wild pansy face your broadcast spell

Of thoughts at ease compatible!
Springs tiny yellow spreading cinquefoil
   In companion red of campion flowers,
To scent of honeysuckle caught in bowers.
   With ragged-robin her late common-flax escapes

Laced with common mouse-ear chickweeds,
   As woodsorrel graceful on the knobbly knees
Of beech! In chorus sing we beneath

Tremendous trees, the Hosts of flowers:
"Oh! Nanny, have we picked *enough* of these?"

Parts 1 and 2 published by the author March, 1977, first edition; May, 1977, second edition. Part 3, published by author with *Notail at Wesley*, Spring, 1977, and November, 1977. Buttercups parts 1, 2, and 3 together in one volume, Summer 1979, hardcover published by Exposition Press, 1980, U.S.A., poems read by author on B.B.C. (Kent) December, 1977, and January, 1978. Further broadcasts planned with author's readings in Kent. Poem above published in *Times* and *Post,* April 14, 1977.

The book now passed the Kent Education Committee for use in schools. Also used by Dr. John Tapia at the Fort Lewis College, Durango, Colorado, for students in the study of English.

Checkmate in Decree Nisi

I crept from the sun to Your shadow—
  it held me! Heard what You wanted to say:
The stroke of the north wind was Your image
  in flurries of red driven may.
The burn of the blossoms in grasses,
  leaves with their heart at my feet—
Here—in the dark of Your shadow—
  my sentence meets Your defeat.

Written in November, 1972.

To My Grandchildren

From His love flows
    the sparkling mellowed wines
as grapes sweet young faces glow . . .
    soft blooms the petal-wise
    of skins
    Grandchildren
akin to glisten of ripe citrons:
    their shining hair
their changing mirrored eyes

Like apple-blooms on snow white linen . . .

Written in Oban, 1973, in December looking at the photographs on the mantlepiece! Prize-winning poem in finals of the Alice Gregory Memorial Comp., adjudicator, Mike Shields, January, 1978. Published in *Orbis,* no. 30; *Poetry International Times* and *Post,* May 4, 1978.

Stuart—Born Nature's Child

BORN NATURE'S CHILD
with city steeps this head
      Wild as town wind
that sweeps through dusty streets
      as schoolboy friends:
a trembling challenge to his friends,
      foes? enemies immature
for dwells in his brave heart a tiger
      born and more . . .

BORN NATURE'S CHILD
versatile boy where sleep is but an end
      from dynamo noise!
Schoolboy who early wakes, rich learning
      finds in life he's king.
An oyster world though frightened when he finds
      His kingdom eggshell thin!

BORN NATURE'S CHILD
"Give me the boy! YES!
      His vivid personality . . ."
"How may we keep him FREE?
      We visualize, yet understand the man?"
Yet easy would it be if not surrounded
      by New World's computers?
Space Seventies' telescopic plans.

BORN NATURE'S CHILD
within a greenbelt a grandchild, old
      Market town now beats her transplant heart,
In giant over-under pass, a town grown to rule too . . .
And my Jack the Giant killer
      trained on his beanstalk
of new-better-letter schools . . .

BORN NATURE'S CHILD
he loves God's nature: lions within parks
      adored dog, tame cat, his rabbits—
but bird within a cage?
      Bars are his torment too, loves curiosities range

WITHIN THIS PERSONALITY

the versatility of knee bent within an ancient
    abbey
curious and silent
    content to bare his raven head in innocence.
I will remember always the way he walked
    his cheeks apple-red, the trembling lip long years ahead—
Brought upon world from heredity to make or break?
While still a minor passions will to cry confused
    Father to the Man
    was this nature's plan?

This heart beats with grandson
    Tiger born and more . . .

Age six years.

Stuart—The Postscript

BORN NATURE'S CHILD,
With city steeps this head
Wild as town wind
and new schoolboy friends . . .
Now passed to the Watford
Grammar School—
this versatile boy where sleep
is just an end . . .

WITHIN THIS PERSONALITY
with the same innocence;
loves, curiosities range again:
"Nanny, will you take all your flowers
so beautiful when you move to Kent?
Will your birds *follow* you, Nanny?
You couldn't leave them behind?
to resent . . .

Age twelve years.

Poem written before the age of the last two verses—age nine—when in the
story of *Butter in the Buttercups.*

A Monday Commuting

Dawn parts the sleep-walking, suburban-red night
   awakens her quick-silver paths in blue veined
       daylight:
Jets streaming to airport vapors the half-world
       asleep
   in dull rumble of train-rock to a new puce-pink week!
Let cradled birds hum on street neon light
   of warm amber perches, to furrowed crow of alarm clocks
now joining the underground's circus of ringed bowlered
       clowns
The *Times, Telegraph,* shield from coughs, jaundiced yawns
   A tousled boredom with mute stares, a Monday commuter's
       dawn:
To golden city engulfing; wheat consuming, brewing storm
   of ulcers, haemorrhages this escalator daily churns its
       Humanity!

Logic daily spills upon a sedulous vast mass
   where city sweeps this secret tide-washed sea;
       Thames
and neat vampires file and smile in a rhythmical dawn
   as autumn rides to halt the heart, tired artery
from leap of frog—snail to its shell
       moon to the sun's pool!
An evening's paved Hades of train sandwiched, ciphered
   and wringing brains in a long train-rack of dreams . . .
A brief acquaintance from a tide of spiked black
       umbrellas
   growing in a living vine, mirrored in a landscape ride
to quick-silver paths: again escapes the city sails
   new mercy of home; family, television, and all its
       Ivory Towers . . .

Watford, 1973. The line from Watford Junction and on . . . a commuting
world as seen with the eye now accustomed to the wilds . . .

It Was As Oban Wings of an Angel

It was dawn's breath overpowered
  powdered white wayward in cloud—
snowcrisp as shore's shell pink kiss
  in a deckle edge of delicateness:

It was a prism of scent
  in twin-bowls blushed hyacinth—
mist filtering the lone room
  rocks their solid perfume:

It was a mirrored path rose
  to a ridged blue of high snows—
in purple glow loch's black dome
  reflected colors the foam:

Filling eye of a child's pensive stare
  imbued my own with nectar—
overpowered from high tenement room
  my laughter rose in ambient bloom:

Bubbling pink as sweet corked champagne
  Winter-ghosts as moon through the rain
It was at the end of this rainbow
  A door-wide welcomes a child angel . . .

In January, 1973, a small child stood looking up at the flat, gazing at the
windowboxes where hyacinth were in bloom in snow showers!

The Crusades

I see a pattern where the world cannot embrace . . .
we weave from tracery of once high boughs
    now—grave-broken twigs of thought:

Buds a new sad universe who cannot retrace
    our spinning time?
        these were the bales spun, yarns from which men
        believed and died . . .

An arctic wind drifts; blowing the red plastic
    poppy-heads from anchored wreath of a cold
    November remembering,
        sun skates and lies

on a steel-bladed sea as within a scored path
    a bloody mirage I see
        Tanks afloat amid a hundred eider ducks
        that swim the bay—

The remembered army "ducks" where mulberry harbors
    dipped and swayed—
        How channel then bore calm in swell, grave risks
        today are graver still:

Armadas now more strikes for pay
    the common market grille . . .
        new coinage purses all lips that find even
        with MORE "twist" can kill:

Dickensian stomachache
    is but a spoon that stirs inflation's wake!
        From golden sovereigns to silver mixed my mind . . .
        Grandchildren will count

Their hundred pence!
    Can it be that they will learn the tricks of time
                        how two
                            + two
                    were always
                            five

How lies are truths? How evil mounts?
That it is not a grave-peace which counts?
Strength would be in disbelief—
Country unite

Where are our new Crusaders,
Cross for peace?

At Oban Bay, N.W. Scotland, February, 1972.

The poem as sent with the *Horizon* magazine to Dr. J. Bronowski in March, 1974. His reply to me in April (he died in August) I quote: "Thank you and best wishes for your book, you may use the poem marked.* I am sorry I have nothing else." His poem follows which was his reply to "The Crusades." Published first in *Horizon* in 1974 and taken from his gift to me of *The Christmas Poetry of the Bronowskis,* the Salk Institute, La Jolla, Christmas, 1973.

Author's note: As I prepare this anthology in 1979 in the middle of strikes in England I can but add ". . . men *believed* in and *died* . . ."

From The Christmas Poetry of the Bronowskis

Blue as a dream and fabulous,
  Suspended between time and space,
Here hangs, immaculate in glass,
  The tropic bubble of the year that's past.

I tip the glass and suddenly
  See the snow in flurries fly:
A trick of weather in a toy
  Shakes my memory with joy.
So winter used to bite and storm
  Raked me long ago and froze me warm.

The book is a selection of Christmas Greetings sent to friends. This poem
was his choice for the poet.

Copyright given April, 1974, Dr. J. Bronowski. Written at La Jolla,
November 15, 1964. Published by S.B. in *Horizon* in my editorial: "Life
through a View Finder."

O Stranger

(Part 1)

APRIL rain like teardrops
    steals the greener lawn

APRIL sunshine peeps so dreamlike
    on journey new begun:

When you confide in me
    O Stranger

With wisdom seek the blossoms bare
    from apple-bough?

Do YOU belong to summer-new
    of full-leaf heart?

From long-searching song
    balm fragrant descant psalm?

Written at Esher, April, 1974. Part 2 at the close of book written at Elstree, April, 1978.

The first meeting with a friend of a friend's which was to have such a great influence on the later years!

Winter Seascape

The sea runs back against itself
  With scarcely time for breaking wave
To cannonade a slatey shelf
  And thunder under in a cave

Before the next can fully burst.
  The headwind, blowing harder still,
Smooths it to what it was at first
  A slowly rolling water-hill.

Against the breeze the breakers haste
  Against the tide their ridges run
And all the seas a dappled waste
  Criss-crossing underneath the sun.

Far down the beach the ripples drag
  Blown backward, rearing from the shore,
And wailing gull and shrieking shag
  Alone can pierce the ocean roar.

Unheard a mongrel hound gives tongue,
  Unheard are shouts of little boys:
What chance has any inland lung
  Against this multi-water noise?

Here where the cliffs alone prevail
  I stand exultant, neutral, free,
And from the cushion of the gale
  Behold a huge consoling sea.

By kind permission of Sir John Betjeman from his *Collected Poems*. On corresponding with the poet in Oban in his letter of 28:11:73 " . . . you may choose one of the sea for your book with best wishes, John B." What better poem than the above when about to commence the sail of the Atlantic!

Correspondence with the poet was in her exile days in Oban when I used to watch J.B.'s programme of English countryside with his poems on T.V. Before he became poet laureate and his letter received October, 1976: "Best wishes for your continued success, J.B."

Impressions of Madeira

To have and to hold

From Seaward is the hazy ridge
    of Mountains
  Sheer from the sea . . .
    I climb to Terreiro da Luta, wind
down in the long toboggan run
    that slides and rakes the cobblestones
Steered by a valiant crew of two . . .

Climbing aboard from Monte
    —"I understood"—
To the terminus at Funchal . . .
    a pound note was their due:
When an old woman shakes her head and fists
    "Wicked" . . . said she . . . "wicked it is,
I lost a son for likes of tourist—Hold You!"

Her English broken, cracked as her voice—
    —toboggan's wickerwork
standing on its downward course . . .
    I closed my eyes to weep
in a mist sea-swept:
    for men I realize a leg have lost
That we in our pleasures seek . . .

From mists that climb the hazy ridge
    at Portela
the Poiso Pass at 4,592 feet
    will hold you in its panoramic spell!
In exaltation of the winding road
    a pearl valley through Machico
to Santa Cruz . . . as vase

Of flowers coral to mauve,
    —frilled and pendulous
Hybrid hibiscus flame on hydrangea carpets—
    in grass verge clover, buttercup and daisy . . .
From shore to shore in breathless feast
    of their colors worked on linen tablecloths
and vivid embroidery on baskets . . .

I lost myself in this hazy ridge
  as pendulous
with this exotic island's magic . . .
  I lost myself in the wine-tasting lodge!
and found Funchal wound in a garland of lace
  which will weave a lasting peace
slow as the carros drawn at oxen pace—

To remember Madeira as a "tourist" . . .

The commencement of sail to the West Indies in which a sequence of poems
follow, chosen from selection and readings given on the *Reina-del-Mar*, P. O.
Line, 1974.

To the West Indies

Now Hold the Sound

NOW HOLD THE SOUND of deep's mystique
Pulse-throb of engine, oceans sleep—
Roll of Atlantic off sealane
As flying fish air-wreath, sea reign
In ship's fairylights reflection; star
and dear moon, shine you upon the fir
I left in sentinel Loch Broom?
Night whistles no Geraldo tune—
His sister's wish—Please remember him
to his favorite of "Huckleberry Finn."

Another famous songwriter from America
prefers at night to keep from "spotlight" stir—
Now two Dames from "Coronation Street"
Rest during day, the cooler night sweep
cobwebs of English television away—
Here is born the true romance of every day!
How dolphin laugh at breakfast hour,
rise, splash to the tune "America!"
St. Thomas left behind we sail—

NOW HOLD THE SOUND — of ship on rail!

Key to each night hear rhythm swell
in flock jewelled robes of each gorgeous belle,
handsome escort float of citadel—
 NOW HOLD THE SOUND of SUNDAY CHAPEL BELL

Author's note: Geraldo's sister heard the sad news of her brother's death
on board ship.

The two ladies from Coronation Street, Julie Goodyear and Jean Alexander,
were travelling together and are looking forward to their poem!

102

In Guadeloupe I Pick a Flower

From Asphodel—

From sugar cane—
alternate flower banana trees
pinks in tropic's green
    I feel
    I hear
Columbus whisper near?

I stupid stare
from lava's lips
into earth's steaming bowel
    and fear
    I feel
rock-tremble, peer

into cauldron cold
I hold on to warmer thought
of one Parisian blanche fleur
    sheathed white,
    silken Fontainebleau
Lily château of Loire!

Here rum punch shouldered
my cold-fingered hold
on a second long-stemmed flower
    waxen white
    Madonna lily
picked here in a wild phantom border

where bull frog croak—
the rain forest road steaming steeps
winds from jostle of the jacamar!
    See rhythmic deep
    sun-drenched beach
a set of sun through palm—

The sheet-dark velvet woos the night
in sea where sweep the blues to greens
in fire of molten mercury pour

```
            moon's ochre
            tropic shore
                              I feel
                              I hear
    Columbus?  whisper near—

    (Asphodel—lily of Greek mythology, plant of the dead!)
```

To the summit of La Soufriere, 4,870 ft., semiactive volcano. Christopher Columbus, 1493; S. B. 1974.

Published in *Envoi,* 22:4:77. "Highly commended," Helen McGowan.

N.B. James Callahan! Prime Minister, 1979.

Trinidad Through a Green Eye

He said:
> "You have the greenest eyes I ever saw . . . "

I smiled
He said:
> "If to your country England came
> You show *me* hospitality, yes?"

I said:
> "Yes"
> and confidently strolled away to choose
>   a cool dress . . .
> The dockside glittered
> shook with lust of modern
>   calypso band!

He followed—
He said:
> "I buy you the dress—
> You like this one?
>   I take you to the beach, yes?"

His black eyes smiled
He whispered:
> "I offer hospitality—yes?"
> Golden fillings gleamed between his ivories!
> My ivory hand held and shook with the black!
> The dockside glittered
> shook with lust of modern
>   calypso band:
> The hot palm fringed in WELCOME
> as *Pilgrimage* I thrust within
>   his hand—

My green eyes smiled
I whispered:
> "*We* give hospitality on both shores—
>   yes?"

1974.

Author's Note: *Pilgrimage,* the anthology of verse which the author had taken on voyage for readings on the P.O. Line, *Reina-Del-Mar.*

"When we allow freedom to ring from every hamlet, from every state and every city, we will be able to speed up that day when all of God's children, black men and white men etc., will be able to join hands and sing in the words of the old Negro spiritual "Free at last . . ."—the late Martin Luther King, the man with a vision and a hope.

Maracas Bay to Robinson Crusoe, Tobago

The journey taken by air from the mainland

COME . . .   join with travel now in "Skyline Highway"
across the Northern Range these modern
pirates three
to Maracas Bay descent . . .

HEAR . . .   palm-fringed shore of legend in infancy . . .
sea—and view the contraband treasure of mystery,
this South Sea Island vision
from crescent flight wing-streaming air

SEE . . .   all sand-golden thought is possible here
on a backcloth sail of olive scenery!
The Crown Point banana surf cream
of Tobago—

FEEL . . .   Robinson Crusoe here with Man Friday!
A legend?
In ultra-violet ray, a mirrored float

TOUCH . . .   fluorescent as fish in rainbow dart
resting between my fingertips—
stark naked, brown as the legend!

I HOLD THE SOUND of liquid rope

and all my childhood dreams telescope
in wave through turquoise cradled I
on palm-stretched shore

ROAR . . .   of all West Indian breakers call
"*Was* Robinson Crusoe—legend?"

São Miguel, or My Flower-White Camellia?

Ponta Delgada to Sete Cidades

"*A casa ideal, se deseja uma lembranca dos Acores . . .*"*
Lunch with the Portuguese
Wine red to please:
Vintro de Cheiro . . .
pineapple with passion fruit—
liquers in basketwork attribute
to fine lace and embroidery—
Native dolls, whalebone carving,
silver filigree
"*Si vous desirez?*"

or My Flower-white Camellia?

Rest? At midday on São Miguel?
Wild as the tall borders with lily Madonna,
scarlet as Vintro de Cheiro!
How deep green are Azores,
how beautiful, mild
in the quill of Feteiras . . .
Poised to thrill in florêt the union of daisy—
English and white with miniature buttercups,
paint the roadside in oils with pink brilliance
Azaleas, all join in wild frenzy
"*Si vous desirez?*"

or My Flower-white Camellia?

Tea-rest on the Island of São Miguel? Oh no!
Climb to the mountain view of the twin crater lakes:
Sete Cidades
from one thousand and seven hundred feet,
where the dark, reflected forest in water far breaks
from a middle rim of the crater!
Here hydrangea
　　　the bordering road
　　　　　brimming with hydrangea.

Spiral back to the coned bushes of tea in plantations,
the village of glass-domed pineapple zones
in spa of a rich, thermal Fernas Valley.

Small native children reach for my purse;
tug at my coat, pull my long hair:
Versing,
I find: *"Ideale Souvenir?"*
The basket, the pineapples spin to the floor
float in the bottle broken of Vintro de Cheiro . . .

In memory of beautiful Borges Botanical Garden:

"Si vous desirez,
                My pressed, now off-white flower
                Camellia?"

*"A good help in selecting a good souvenir from Azores."

Author's Note: Many flowers picked in Azores and the Caribbean were
pressed into a book and have retained their beauty.

The Caroni Swamp: Sanctuary of the Scarlet Ibis

Phenomena of "Roost in the Afternoon"

Six miles to "ROOST IN THE AFTERNOON"
as the temperature rose to a hundred and twenty degrees—
we, encased toe to head, protected from swamp mosquitoes
where water dark oozed between boards green of canoes:
I remembered Paul Robeson's long canoe flotilla
in a wonderful film called *Sanders of the River*—
when ducking from the arrows from bow's sheet forest of water;
canoes in a winding stench, creeping as snakes around stout shoes
as temperature rose, zigzags as jack snipe out of gunshot wound
wind to a hundred and forty degrees . . .
Five miles to "ROOST IN THE AFTERNOON."

"Until we reach the journey's end . . . " so sang Paul Robeson
and in my head where my scalp jungle sweat-froze, *no* halcyon
when a neighboring limb low on tree moaned from the damp heat's
      throne. . .
In underleaf tone of lowering leech! One frail craft leaked a dull monotone:
the Guide's pidgin English of *"Please* keep your seat!"
With four miles to "ROOST IN THE AFTERNOON"
The crocodile sleep . . .
as the temperature rose, feint water rose as an odd paralytic spirit plumed
as sun tired lay her head on a forest humid-dyed red!
Crimson died amid reek of decay in a cold-wild shriek of an animal lone . . .
Three miles to "ROOST IN THE AFTERNOON"
Four—five—six—seven-thirty in fire-bowl of sun
This journey is done . . .
The battery of jungle wings like great rubies grew into an IBIS brilliance
As giant butterfly kings and queens settle to roost in a mammoth séance,
their scarlet upon scarlet exotically beautiful wings spin
as moth drawn through a new crimson eye of moon!
Canoes rock, for this is a day of pride not opinion!
My clothes wringing wet, with sock and shoe divest . . .
O! Will I return to this earth-womb and forest?
From note of the hummingbird, my yellow bird of banana trees,
valley of pastel pink orchids, brilliant oceans, palm with the breezes?
Contrast where the IBIS roost, now canoes threading their way
      like swamp needles,
here magnified as the eyes of binoculars feeble—
Dark—and inky dark in a six-mile journey back

Black—black down on the hostile spill of jungle!
I remember the guidebook said, "SEE THE IBIS ROOST"
Six miles out—six miles back
                    ROOST IN THE AFTERNOON?
                              Not I
                         —In loom of sound—
                    and jungle-wonder . . .

A journey to see the ibis at sundown, the time for roosting being debatable!

Bouquêt from Alfonso of Navarre

HOW to interpret love?
Are flowers essence of the moment beyond speech?
I found the inscription floral, written unique

"Con todo cuanto mas guapo para
la señora . . ."

An interpreter I found when port we reach—
HOW to interpret love?
Are flowers moments in time that fade obsolete?
In closing eyes did Alfonso into depths
    of Proteus' sleep?

HOW to interpret love?
"Notwithstanding their beauty they are more
beautiful because they are for the lady . . ."
When the ocean liner has sailed
And the posy fragrance from Spain
Lies dormant, yet so powerful at my feet
Are all flowers essence of the love
    beyond our reach?

Towyn

Morning mist rises as the soul of God
   gently whispering in competition
with the silken flow of a gray sea
   as arms which hold us competently!

Sun rises on cool-blue with cotton clouds
   of spun marigolds
and dapples sea, the wary fish and fluted sand
   in a miniature whirlpool swell

From night's first sunburst of bass fishing!
   Surfing in darkening conditions
of sun ablaze through a night curtain cloud—
   a dance of scarlet centuries aflame

Remembering the names of invaders
   from Ireland, Scandinavia—
Pages in enduring faith of pilgrims
         —TO TOWYN—

As the ebbtide pools spread far and wide
   in preaching of Crusades below
the towering Cader-Idris range
   Fellowship as deep as Mary Jones*

Who walked the Llanfihangely Pennant
   In 1880 to Bala!
The firm beliefs from known to unknown
   glows in script across a glowing heaven—

Messages to all to find life
   through a view finder—
written in skies vermillion and gold
   in the vast rise
      set of sun
        AT TOWYN . . .

*At the age of sixteen Mary Jones walked the mountains bare of foot to buy a Bible; the forming of the British and Foreign Bible Society.

Written on my second visit to Towyn. The second poem to be published was written at the Baptist Fellowship Holiday Home and published in 1970 entitled "Thoughts on a Fellowship Holiday." Encouraged to write by the minister Rev. Paul Mortimore, and my first book, *Pilgrimage,* is dedicated to him.

113

The River Dysynne

Gone Fishing

(To Dan)

Only the mallard ducks when disturbed
   fly to a safer height above our tireless feet
through gorse tough, dank-tall and whispering
   grass framing our soft speech.
Above the curtain crowd of butterflies
   the Argus Brown and Silver-Studded Blues
their rippled compliment to flower
   of Harebell and myriad citizens Heather-new:

Mother Mute Swan with fish breathe where silence
   tolls supreme in pastures where thoughts
completely lost in visions of fish—
   swimming—swimming—swimming
away from sight to tease and bask below the beech,
   where God has hand painted every shade—
from needle of the Lesser Sharp Sea Rush and blade
   and pale brown flowers of sun-kissed

Bird, bee-fingered, river-red and amber hollow!
   The early Whooper Swan-etched sky in loom of cloud,
the wing and sigh of fishing rod and trout!
   Wary fish rise on a river-ring of butterfly
as Wood-White skate on Nature's colorslide.
   Sedgewarbler, moorhen, mallard and duck eider
are out-watching moments long in shadow of sea trout . . .

The water screams—
   with rod taut, line and reel of fisherman Dan
reaps fish—fish skims from depth to water edge
   gill radiates, the eye fluorescent flounce—
now boggled steel ready beside its instrument Death:
   "Twelve pounds or ten?"—as silver slid
back to the waiting mallard duck, the wonder world of fish . . .

We smiled: "I was going to put it back," he said
   in capture of a reward that's richer . . .
Richer than the silver spin of river
   and tireless as the heroism—fish

As the poem is dedicated to my eldest son, a fisherman since a teenager,
I must add he is an excellent fisherman! And with the wit and humor of
"fisherman's tale"—out in all weather!

Mountain of Decree Absolute

NO—I couldn't return to you now
YOU would see me as I am
   changed, only my laugh—
   my cry remains the same,
   sometimes beckoned by
   an abstract cough . . .
YOU would look into my green eyes
   where now would be serenity
   of innocence?
   Flame of an instant erection
   the burning of perfection?
YOU would look into my soul
   blue eyes soaring
   to heights where love
   now my sweet fame
   winged from the work and toil
   of marriage,
   never shall this be shame . . .
NO—I couldn't return to you now
   though quietly still
   my children
   and I bear your name.

"Climb every mountain . . ."

A Brief Encounter

Bloomsbury Square

The short grass tufts refreshing after the hot streets
    as dusty, tired I sit upon my Welsh coat new of tweeds . . .

Listening to the continuous traffic's roar
    watching the children play, London sparrows flit and soar . . .

Colored play of ball and pigeon swoop gathering sandwich crumbs
    this different peace of Bloomsbury Square becomes

The glade between me and the world out there
    as I swivel on the short grass tufts in halcyon moment bare . . .

As your feet . . . "Were you footsore, too?" as quietly you stare,
    were your secret thoughts drowned in dust and traffic roar?

"May I share a few moments with you, please?"
    You tiptoe as sunshine through a storm cloud tease . . .

We talk—small talk—I felt you did not wish to pry—
    instead you asked my name; why, oh, why! did I feel an urge
    to cry?

You shook my hand briefly, almost roughly said: "My name is
    Roy . . ."
    the happy moment fades, flees in a memory from joy.

Traffic is all I see, the dust and roar in opened wound
    smothers your warmest smile, how could you know the sound

Of another's name; your own, could bring me pain? Lost peace in
    Bloomsbury Square—
    I crossed alone the busy thoroughfare . . .

A glade between you and the busy world out there—
    He died where swallow fly in gossamer cloud where meditation
    flower . . .

August, 1974. It did materialize *only* in the way that I learned the new friend
was a son of a well-known publisher.

As Sparks of Humor Dart Through Shadowed Hill

Where Strophe Watersmeet

As sparks of humor dart through shadowed hill discreet—
and dune where strophe Watersmeet

I miss those creatures of the sea
the seals I knew by name implicitly!

The herring gull fed each day from eager hand,
my sad and hooded crow with merriment understands—

Beside the Loch each beckoning whooper swan
at dawn's break waits for daylight crumb.

Brown eider duck each calling Autumn
in fellowship with Lorne and Crinnan

Sunning fleet of grey lag geese
the set pearl of Oban Bay repletes?

Now to accept each transient scene
as sparks of humor dart through memorial mountain queens—

A morning quiet-cool in damp mist
drowns in the eerie foghorn of this ambient retreat,

Reflections part in the cold jade of channel—
can I see unity with this sweet Watersmeet?

Here, where I am home with swallow, blackbird, thrush—
here, as native lost among England's greener marsh?

Stark my thoughts as mute swan her choric singing
alone with solitary curlew and hills of pebbled beach weeping . . .

Watching the stoic path of ochre harvest moon
as in a bloodstream pours God's sacred heart and soon

As sparks of humor dart through shadowed dune—
lifting the latch of dawn's tapestry surround in one

117

I creep in unity with Oban Bay—the Cinque Ports continent
unique in humorous dart are shadows of hill where
Strophe Watersmeet.

Published in *Envoi,* 1970.
Examiner, Pain, "A poem of depth and sincerity."

A "watersmeet of mind" achieved after return to live again in Kent from
Oban, Argyllshire.

The Cross

From Minaret—To Bunny

When your loved one turns away
   the pain and rejection whatever reason—
a hole bores within the heart
   leaving it to convey treason . . .

into those small, dark hours creep pride
   as wakeful hours drift and question sweet
revenge? Where memories built in ivory towers
   and wretched only find bitter deceit . . .

In the deep pain of the minaret and flame
   of love betrayed with another's kiss
Can now our severed souls gather their threads?
   for now the dream impossible is this.

Author's note: The following poems are "Rejection," "A Symphony Un-
finished," "Shipwreck of Yesterday," "Where Swallow Fly," and "Put-
ting Back the Clock"—in sequence one of the most traumatic in the poet's
life, and second only to divorce.

With the death of not only "the impossible dream" but—of the friend.

119

Rejection

When finally I saw the reflected truth
   within your eyes; brown now, devoid of pain
liquid with powers to hypnotize yet pool
   my balmy invasion of your time!
The pledge is broken, my dear, now, no veil—
   but plasma drawn: no book together bound,
O volumes apart where only leaves transmit
   and fall from library's chapter reminiscent:

Then, why swallow I bitter all my pride?
   Dare to invade your sanctuary of glass?
Behind this wicker gate another page in fate
   and burdened trespasser I kneel unafraid
of the channel where your true heart *must* speak—
   for your shield now from love is but a toss
of blanket and in its fold so surely dies—
   as from your couch and sick the death of
      moment lies . . .

So dies my need, my burning urge to hold—
   to clothe you with the comfort of my words—
Instead these words transform and taper knife edge—
"Oh, no, I didn't love you . . . " *You* mustn't weaken
(remember your soft curl at nape of neck?)
and *she*, stranger to you, you said:
" . . . had saved my life from accident and death"

For she could reject her pride too—
   and both would leave your couch instead?

Boston, 1974.

120

A Symphony Unfinished

Strangely it was your weakness
    I loved most . . .
bends as the soft curl at nape of neck,
    the chin in stubble
        stubborn yet
your eyes always reflect my mountain's mist—

Brown as deep lochs when troubled
    I loved most . . .
where waters run in secret giving of cool
    exclusive love—
        contrasting kiss
and burning as in troubled heat

The dream impossible—
    I loved most
firm arm and short in a quick turn of wrist
    "clasp your hand in mine"
            in duet we said,
Now an eternity hangs on a thread

As the river tolls to the sea
    I loved most,
here in the English mist hangs your lifeline . . .
    Our exile world
        shines as the curl,
your weakness sounding in your illness

Stubborn yet . . .
    the symphony unfinished?
I loved most not the lustre of each embrace,
    the chin in stubble!
        but all the burning yesterdays
shall be *my symphony — your wish*?

August, 1974.

Shipwreck of Yesterday

WAVES
    splash quietly upon the shore
THE SEA
    rhythmically confides in me
        so softly to assure

Sweeping a fringe of flotsam, jetsam
    jettisoned like thoughts spiral ring
    of lonely stone monograms,

As the mind where calmer water shelters
    and stores reflected, ripple mackerel skies!
        Tell me miracle water

How you send the problems drifting by?
    Shall we ask the fisherman as trembling catch
    a late admiral butterfly?

Truant wings of summer-late swallows cry,
    so mystery stirs within a seashell.
        Ocean music lies

In surge of tide, cascades in laughter
    where a winsome child at play, hair caught
    with sunshine's copper

In a foot-pool float of pebbles streaming,
    gleaming sands stealing crablike from the bay
        Tortuous romancing

Town child counting seashells lullaby—
    as squirrel-like she combs ebb tides
        in the Shipwreck of Yesterday . . .

Littlestone, 1974.

Poem also adjusted to contain the day looking after a Vietnamese child and published in 1980, *Women's World*.

122

Where Swallow Fly

WHERE SWALLOW FLY
  over all the many colored seas
I, from travelling Caribbean's
    thunderous waves transfuse
      this present scene, vivid in screen
        from eye as sheen of sun
          disappears between gossamer cloud
          The Flower of Meditation!

Your ears may hear this heart beat alone
  in bosom's near-gray of Littlestone?

GOOD-BYE MY LOVE
  in oldest harbor's memory repose

Your eyes so softly from me now close
    liquid the brown and lidded white—
      Death retains her own mellow light
        where swallow in their hundred clown
          perform on tired grin of old seawall
            where fission of home, Caribbean fall . . .

WHERE BURN OF WING
  cleaves to tarmac gray

Waves thunderous in Romney Bay
  —how twin-tides kite-silver retrospect
    as swoop of island's loop-fringe magnificent!
    Here duet firm shares shore-kissed shore
    and makes the parting mirror
          —ALL—
      from tall palm tree to Marsh poppy horned:

ON WINGS OF SOUND
  we shall share the channel flight—
    our pathways joined
      in strength of unity
        Vision gains perfect sight

        WHERE SWALLOW FLY
        DEATH retains her own mellow
        —LIGHT—

Putting Back the Clock

PUT BACK THE CLOCK . . .

    fate cannot explain
      when love dies twice,
        how the stained sword
          turns scarlet
            blood rushing from the wounds . . .

First it was a youth's cry to me

    in an unknown monsoon—
      sunbursts from the flesh
        the floods kissing
          as the waters of tropical storm . . .

I was young in the "low rack" of storm cloud

    chasing each other
      higher and higher
        steeping, mounting,
          reaching—attaining
            an impossible dream!

I was young but the years drew their sunset

    came the unutterable silence
      the put back the clock of divorce—
        fate cannot explain
          why love's born again

As a chord chosen from a musical romance?

    the theme is chosen
      From, not for the heart . . .
        the sound of many instruments
          the impossible dream, apart?

The secret strings will accompany me through the glens—

    Then softly as a velvet curtain
      drapes in purple caress

                the mountain pulse
             contains the message
                of your early death . . .

I was still young, but late in my middle age

        when the ghosts reappear,
           wade through the monsoon
           flame through the glen
             in fire-dancing light

PUT BACK THE CLOCK . . .
                You gain an extra hour tonight.

October Moonlight on Dungeness Point

OCTOBER MOONLIGHT shall ride
    above her sheer silvered channel in light,
beam-buoyant my feet treading the trapeze
        to tap dance upon high wires nautical romance
Foams crescendo of crests tumble with satanic ease:

OCTOBER MOONLIGHT shall ride
    keeping distance from menacing shadows
tide-gaze into crystal depths in a treadwheel of white,
        vibrant stoned beach drags in myriad bottled questions
in resonant-deep and desolate voice . . .

OCTOBER MOONLIGHT shall ride
    wrapt in a sea-mist blanket her return kiss of Dungeness
sheet-wed in moonlight, O ride I in starlit chorus—
        O ride I new paths where dawn's moonlit daughter is born
sharing this swift coral cradle of seas treacherous,
        tremulous calm of my October
            blue's symphony . . .

1974.

As in poem "Symmetry," the transformation given by light. " . . . as Death
sans fear one HEARS the turn of tide." As in Life also; the author suf-
fered a severe fall just before the poet's dinner. The Cinque Ports Poets
Society being founded by the author but through the following illness the
society, then worldwide, accepted the poet's retirement and was followed
by a local society only, the Romney Marsh Poets. The magazine *Horizon,*
published and edited by the author, ran for two years worldwide and with
many famous contributors adding their prose and poetry.

The Cinque Ports Poets Dinner, 1974

In Chorus with Our Fred . . .

In Unity:
where church bells their Christmas peace-ring
in the practicing meadows of eve'
our car speeds through the marshland mist to festivity
for the second annual celebration of Cinque Ports Poets!
Last year at the Plough Inn in merrily packed Romney banquêt—
now to dine at the renowned Mermaid Inn of ancient Cinque Ports
endows thirty seven members with pride in Rye!

All friends, members who wished to meet with Christmas spirit
    prophesy—
sharing individual readings from works newly featured in magazine
Horizon . . .
Their merriment finally caught in a request poem from
                    Councillor Raymond:

Pray Silence:
for His Worship the Mayor of New Romney . . .
In a dramatic scene he accompanies us
a pajama-clad guide through his: "Traumatic dream experience of his
    early demise!
The consequential civic repercussions of his death . . . "
Related and dram-streamed to feather our amusement,
wine-washed to add to our equal poet's relish
But not of *his* untimely death!
Oh, no! Our Fred is not an *ordinary bard*
For have you not read, or heard?
His ballad sad, the sudden death of one betrothed blackbird?
Where his related story true of the country courting pairs in mate?
How she in song beautiful was struck down by a hurried driver's race?

Pray Silence:
for our Fred brings real tears to eyes of Romney Marsh—
His poem, "The Widower," took pride of place in *Horizon* last!
To quote him in all melancholy:
" . . . and as he watched his loved one die
    a tear I vow slid from his eye;
    If this were to happen to you or me
    Imagine the hue and cry there'd be!
    So why destroy beauty placed here for us
    Or silence a voice in dawn's spring chorus?"

127

Pray Silence:
   for His Worship the Mayor of Rye . . .
   His smiling gaze and glass raised to apologize?!
      "*No* poet he . . . " yet his speech wound with ceremonious
wit,
      his toast:
      "To true wisdom in the great cultural contribution
      made to the community by societies such as
                  the Cinque Ports Poets!"

In Unity:
   where church bells for Sunday matin's ring
   in the practicing meadows of morning—
   the clarity across the cobbled streets in Rye
   of a morning of cars packed with international
                  —poets—
   Down to the whistling marsh from the parapet
   I call and wish:

      " . . . Friends, please slow the pace
      Remember our Fred's poetic epitaph:
      May I quote?

      "On lichened post this blackbird cock
      With head held high and breaking heart . . .
      As sexton dressed to play his part
      Surveyed his love with eyes forlorn
      Her shattered wing and body torn,
      And as he watched his loved one die
      A tear I vow slid from his eye;
      If this were to happen to you or me
      Imagine the hue and cry there'd be . . . "

As blackbirds:
   in tryst we in celebration then would miss
   the friendship, the spring,
   one poem and one voice
   One romance—one wing
   In a coming year's breath of dawn chorus
   or our SILENCE . . .

Christmas Dawns on Romney Marsh

From midnight service at St. Nicholas Church, outside to the dawn's hoar frost, and the Celebrated Birth

From midnight carols
 and all the Norman cloistered
  prayers
   with Christmas Eve quiet

Now amidst all beautiful beamed
 moonlight
  a mullioned window torch
   in driven shaft of light—

It's light tight clenched
 between my hand
  in arrow pulse and forage
   on old and worn stones

Flagging and steps to white-dusted ground,
 bearing the crib's Christmas message
  a gnarled tree finger-points
   in natural bare branched shade—

So His brilliance shines
 in frosts merriment of palm
  of all limb
   in a wild knife of life's east wind!

Here a filigree ring
 of mellow earth and bell teeth
  of belfry chime in dawn's hoar frost:
   from midnight chimes

Romney to Bethlehem swaddling Birth
 the warmth of universe,
  in a clear-cold whispered
   carol and psalm.

The illustration is the interior of St. Nicholas Church, New Romney, taken from an old postcard and illustrated by Roland Portchmouth.

A Rustle in the Rain

Between the rustle in the rain
outside—
and the building of the coal and log fire
inside—
I peered into my mirrored face
swathed
in its bandages and sore!
I felt as the brass clock in retrospect
glass case expressionless,
I broke that too before the war!

In the winged armchair
I settled—
"Stay in bed," the doctor firmly said
stitched—
skillfully my eye and forehead,
gouged
pendulous eye riveted in blue-black.
An ex-naval doctor, when he grinned
in charm of happy rolls of fat:
"Look for yourself," he sat back—

There hadn't been time for an anaesthetic,
I peeped—
beneath the swathed bandages
rimmed—
The forehead hollow as a saucer,
a bloody
eye as cup and saucered
patterned ball, flame and blues indigo!
It was midnight on Sunday
Between the rustle in the rain:

The accident had happened
"Sure . . . " said I—
with Monday morning bleak at eight, his question
answered—
"I *know* I should have called you before,
I was alone
when I did "come round" it was nearly four . . . "
I build up the fire

it all seemed like something from a film
about an infant I once saw:

In mind identical, three weeks long: Outside
inside—
the building of the rustles in the dark
momentarily—
Quiet . . . throbbing now in pain
the forehead
mauve from sickness sucking at my blood dried
into stitches, as questioning eyebrows
in conference raised: " . . . the right frontal?
they had said! Shall I clearly remember life's
pattern again?

When the blackness built up to barrier wall
I know—
only that was the moment of the fall,
words—
in rivers ran wide between me, blood
and floor:
"Can anyone hear me?"
It seems a year ago, yet here am I
white-flowering in bandage
throwing my words to those nameless—

All the wild woods of my spirit world!
Speechless—
tongue-dry to reach for tablets murmuring
I ride—
on cushions of the heather-sweet and prickly moors.
I sleep
a lot—I bleed now only
for the precious tomorrow-time,
for time that's lost I must resign—
and with the poet's Christmas dinner over:

Courage to telephone or write—"O Stranger"—
Will he—
understand the willow "pendent"
Welcome—
me and say once more: "Do come indoors?"
Wide,
high and handsome as his house is . . .

and he? Mature as his screened garden
Glossy with holly, smiling trees and vine . . .

A kindred spirit whispering then:
O STRANGER—
Take I the plunge now to deepest water
FAITH —
with the Master's key still with me
HOPE
to unlock new and changing doors!
Though the shock runs still the bodies actions,
lazy brain is sore—
Shall: "April rain as teardrops steal this greener lawn?"

"Knock and it shall be opened unto you,
Seek—
and ye shall find . . . "
Can he the bridges cross, rivers turbulent
of mind?
Passes this six months and still the stiffness
of suntan over pallor shines.
Tense as if in master mould
or metal cast . . . but he is kind . . .

Burden I share of his divorce
Confides —
He now with me fully! His worn, but other cross—
One who—
in sickness died, left now far behind.
Occult; swollen still,
pain-trembling in warmer days interchanged migraine
I hide behind his graciousness
and my lens polarize.

We stagger to the distant hills
Complacent—
Warm in Scottish sunrise;
Stifling—
and morose return to supermarkets
bright neon glares!

Yet with love I find in softer rains
a living leisure in a deck chair
of new brain—

133

Yes! There's sunlight on a lawn greener—
A reality of dream fairer—
Fine—Clearer

—RUSTLE IN THE RAIN—

In November, 1974. The poem relating to the poet's previous fall and subsequent events which followed, 1975.

Line 10 relating to poems "Tomorrow" and "O Stranger."

June Half-Light in Glen Orchy

3 A.M., 1975

Secret of all
from twilight bewitched
in swirling half-light mist . . .
Glen Orchy foams
in river streaming
tall and weaving
as a night-green ghost
concealing
Secret of all

Bullfinch and lark
herring gull's trout
snow bunting's weed-seed
Cathedral-rise skies
sun's marigold trees,
boughs' shadows reach
to secret skate
a sheep's descent

we, secret all
bathe in the river's bend
a rainbows end
in crystal falls . . .
awake with nature's
great and small
the Secret of Glen Orchy
          —Magical—

Norman Hidden of *New Poetry:* "Good, flowing as the river" (16:8:76).

Revisiting the Highlands with "The Stranger" (refer to poem "O Stranger").
Three poems chosen from those written follow, 1975.

At Wesley

(Thought taken from Matthew 5)

This lovely garden here enclosed
in trembling leaf
of green on velvet's green unfold
Life as it throbs from early sheath
in quiet murmur nature's pattern
unfurls in vivid rose.

A symmetrical screen
a flowered focus holds the eyes
transfixed in a solitary,
realistic moment
when born of reality bears bliss—
is this the dream that's stranger
to the kiss?

Impossible? yet in a soft dream
from sigh as gloss on holly,
bearing her low cool crown of shrub
chases through the sycamore in folly
where robin undisturbed sings love:

From greener myrtles here enclosed
in trembling leaf
I realize this dream
—is cast beyond the mote—

The garden at Elstree, which the author had fallen in love with when visiting "O Stranger"—before going to the West Indies. Again a vision in symmetry this time in foliage . . . revisited at the "Stranger's" invitation, 1975.

137

The Overcoat Man

Warm, tucked up tight
    Ken rests, tunes into night
with slumber snores
    as polestar pours
her solitary light:
    Morning breathes
her mists above the river trees
    Ken turns when I
still lost in lullaby
    from night-magic half-light ply
in Scottish sunrise, ball of fire
    caress blue mountain tops higher
than car and man's serene harmony . . .
Day-fans him into brewing tea " . . . darling
    no sound? except a gull white winging—"

as bee sings cooking stove . . .
    Ken contemplating river's rove
and in his eye ripples silver
    of wood and hilltop quiver,
I as natural to the scenery
    in nude. Bathing prophesy
my gentle overcoat man
    welcome traveller's artisan
with delicious and strong tea!

Refresh him now on
    double eggs and bacon
Range-beans steaming on horizon
    where in contemplation of river
sees he between the traveller and silver!
    This his Soul as unlike stout overcoat discarded

bare in leafed branch reflected
    Man's elusive bird the stowaway
from world, as river runs toward midday . . .
    From wingéd thought: brown rainbow trout
all one in beauty of the Truth he sought—
    not in swiftness of the river
or in tranquil depth of thought
    but as the Spirit

in a drawing-down of mind
    shimmers in its tenderness
WHERE, but in our green Glen Orchy find?

1975. Poem "Highly commended," *Envoi,* 1976.

Between the Lochs

24 Hours between the Red Hills of Skye

The Evening Hills
Reflected in a mirrored haze
          where brown trout rise

The stillness broken only
by a skylark
          where sheep softly graze

The Red Hills laze
Yet silently their promise keep
          of morning's half-light

with tomorrow's pleasures
deep-wrapped in burning heat
          Her morning's sleep—

June, 1975. Perfect peace on the Isle of Skye . . . in brilliant light of sun
and moon.

Where a Primrose Will Ring

(By Duntrune Castle—Poltalloch Estate)

Brambles kneel, creep to loch's water edge
wind whips high color to cheeks of salt
        sea pinks . . .

late blackberry blossoms shelve on evening's tide
and in the forest cool-ripple with elusive
        birds wild . . .

Now is the moment of thought fruitful: flowers
as brambles kneel, crisp with the leaf died red—
a white aconite sleeps in the shadow of night
        blanketed . . .

The saffron plough in early rough snow
as swift in the high scream of polar wind
brambles kneel, clinging to crevice, nest
        in the brae

Where a primrose will ring . . .
from the autumnal blush of all lovely
        transient things . . .

Poem with "Outposts."

A return . . .

No. 7. The Chase

A Testimonial to Mary and Dan—Six Indian Summers in a Watford Garden

An Autumnal Suburban Sunset, 1969

As Summer—petals form her youth-cup,
  a-flower of scarlet paints on evening skies—
her late curl of blossom on canvas weans
  a-soft peach bloom
as skies unfurl rose flesh
  in a nipple-sweet caress—
Rain steals as panther to her young on earth—
  petal-white as milk to the new baby grass,
early frosted garden renews her glory
  in fire of a smoking Heaven's
    gently succored morass:

Between these skies the cradle rise
  of—BUTTER IN THE BUTTERCUPS

A Twin Autumnal Sunset, 1975

May Summer's still bloom—
  as your brilliant blue
    Cornflowers—
in-tuned over the shortened blades of grass—
  blue-domed towers in earth's early Winter's day
darker sepalled mauves
  here honeybees obey—as late;

Where grandchildren, dog and I comb nearby
  WHIPPENDELL—
how Mother-green curls chamfered leaves
  in an early cradle—
mellow as garden's gems—russet pears after-glow,

As clustered Autumn swings her russets
  to Winter's deepest yellow—
flame from all golden range of Buttercup
  where children pair in swing,

143

wing as laburnam seed—
In a flame cloud born of storm's retreat
  a-near thunder-beat
  as roll-call from an Exile's heart
     "A Thank-you, Dan and Mary,
       for my six Indian
         summers . . . "

Period in which the book *Butter in the Buttercups* was written.

November Clad

Who is he? When quiet walks the stair
Plaid-gown tread no multimillionaire
yet wears with steps of life his crown?

Pure sound is he! A diamond stylus
As on the amplifier controlled silence
blue eyes closed, hears in precision?

In projection of an upper class
A clear-cut look, eyes often pierce
the progress of an age in recession!

Security entirely not with bank
More in serenity of pride, frank
in his solidarity no reflection

Of gown and top coat threatened,
Love of surprise this uncontrived
cult in male perfection . . .

His admiration: native Gloucester—
The 'shires and stiles will never tire
His love of new loch's crown's resurrection . . .

1975.

The day on which the author was asked to stay permanently at Wesley.

Petals of Sleep

Crowns not her head when heartbeat night from thorn—
  Quiet of Man who walks this early stair?
Bliss her sleepy head of inspiration
  Love born on truth, wisdom of sharing rare—
For he gives not for return confession
  Of mind's shared peace, this is love's gain to pair!
It was no dream when gentlest thoughts thus join—
  (Hope left his life with wound of knife depth theirs—)
In meditations coin of care with fire
  Of faith; new hope from deeper wells, despair!
With ripening days autumnal wish inspire—
  Later moments flower: Heart's sepals prepare
In waking cherish petal serene desired—
In sleep embrace, cotollary aspired.

January, 1976.

The "O Stranger" experiencing the trauma of early stages in divorce.

146

Soliloquy in August

There is in structure of late rose
   subtle protection of harsh thorn!
There is in a rich wheatfield stand
   a high risk of gale force violent storm.

There is one man I know walks tall
   though slower gait, slight shoulder bent
Wears no protective outward thorn—
   His wisdom, quietness blend
Into golden wheatfield: risen August
   in down-to-earth harvest apple-charm
Of my man's russet cloak, straight eye
   calendar ascent a pensioner becalm . . .

"O Stranger" and now the book *Butter in the Buttercups* is dedicated to
"The Knight on the White Charger."

Remembering Haresfield Beacon

Gloucester

Take not the birdsong
  lest death
infuse us with its stronger breath;

take not the hillrise
  where I prayed
may two again climb sustained;

take not the wild wind
  intermittent rain
rainbow spring: melodious change

take not? these scents
  of early grass,
cool blade shade, amber sun's flower mass!

Take now this cross
  from shepherdess knee—
through a glass darkly see . . .

Nature's patterned range
  perfected burn
of mellowed leaf, swallow wing born

of sunset: glow free
  her altar shed
with pulsing lemon light sacred

in thought bereft,
  heart-lost in prayer—
keep still each bird song duet where

in spring's warm cradled tongue
   her love serenade
winter through faith shall not fade!

Infuse us with song
   lest death
spiral hills prayer in renewed breath . . .

Written at Wesley over the period 1974-1976.

Relates to poem "O Stranger," 1974, and the now shared experience of awaiting his divorce.

Visions White of New Year

WHITE sunlight's splendor shone
    across my hearth
where room dismissed of fir tree
    pine and earth—
scent of needle—wood smoke
    of heath,
wined blossoming of friends
    new and old
whispers in a strange manger
    of new year,
clear frosted moonshine
    sweeps the naked night
O January, were you born
    ever more quiet?

TODAY: first day—
    a Nor-West cherry pink cloud—
Oh yes! Your mood is mine:
    the black as grapes
ripen upon the vine
    sparkling as a toast
in effervescent wine:
    in twelve short hours
a gray stillness moves
    to breathe again—
a tormenting wind proves
    clockwise this vintage
pours like rain, her tears
    in a white lightning—
a thunder roll—
    the barrel of wise
        years . . .

January, 1976.

Written after entertaining very good friends from Watford.

Snowdrops

I MUST GO ON
 now to this living end—
Who dwells in dull despair
 shall force the river's bend—
where in the innerself
 the flow as river to the sea?

A joint pair
 must grasp this secret
of Soul who lives there
 as quietly beside me pure
bunched as snowdrops
 in crystal by this armchair:

I MUST GO ON
 from individuality beware—
now as the pattern change
 of born again!
This waxen flower who wears
 as snowdrops pure
her sleet-green deckle edge,
 dropping delicately sure perfume rare
lost with her secret snow-bouquêt share—

Where she could be one
 but for Affinity
Nature and the Universe!
 In winter sun's caress
now smoke-white in candlelight
 I FEEL her petal soft
beneath breath of Absolute—
 her crystal stemmed
  brave bloom
  —of Death—

Wesley, January, 1976.

The sharing.

The Bowler Hat

Shoe's lace—old, stretched, torments great age
Of eighty year's or more. Black bowler hat
Immaculate; seems out of place: a cage
Surround to wrinkled face, gray hair coin—sat
In fringèd mat below a brim as stiff
As moth-old overcoat in melton
So cumbersome! It would be a sin if
We should pry: bag's heavy plastic question
Our right to stare? Sharp blue-bag eyes brought
Hard lumps into my throat; quick steel of war
In haunting smoke and pain. Were medals sought?
His limbs intact? Gaunt privilege of poor
Where only knowledge left his bowler wore!

Near St. Albans Cathedral, March, 1976.

Published in *Poetry International, Ipse, Envoi,* and the *Times* and *Post,* 1976.

This *Is Constancy at Eastertide*

At OBAN
1971

THIS then the moment of new resurrection
this then the moment complete? A haven rest
where polestar guides the constant heart
through shadowed boughs and tempest?

HIS strong hand quietly led from stoic pride
this unknown chart in life's hermitage path:
this cherished dream as a forgotten fringe
of rain! Remains the sorrowing climb
as organ pipes in requiem! Good Friday's hinge
THIS resurrection wing of life's lovely day
in Spring:

To NEW ROMNEY
1974

THIS then the moment of our sepulchre
finding this love where *no* stone may swing—
to release a tombed heart? Honor; pain, divide
between these cool rushing waters I
harken to my far distant lover, for no silent
martyr this His strong hand leads me from stoic
pride:

To ELSTREE
1975

THIS then the moment of a new resurrection?
As organ pipes in requiem! Good Friday's hinge
in finding this love where another's heart had
—Divided—
THIS is no cool rushing water in a silent fringe
of olive green trees! I find Communion
—Resurrection bread—
THIS wine of life's lovely Easter Day
with Spring!

In the spring of 1975 the author had been asked: "Will you stay until after
Easter"—with the slipping of an engagement ring upon the finger . . .
the poem is now completed in retrospect.

Verse 2 completed the poems pages 119-125 in the fullness of their loss—
no resurrection, 1975.

An Introduction to "Oak House"

April-May Memory Lanes from Lydney-Brockweir

They say: "Give credit where it's due . . . "
This poem then for friends Guy and Hugh:
Our introduction to a delicate first menu
Diviners with a bouquêt garni, wine in
      candlelight tempo . . .

Their choice in both of connoisseur correct
As in their guidance 'round Gloucester lanes perfect!
In early spring's drought year of retrospect
We found bluebell whirlpools ablaze on hill's abyss—

As Guy's imagination gourmêt of the tranquil mind,
With garden produce herbs select alkaline:
With Hugh's prismatic versatile wine of hedgerow,
      dandelion . . .
Kissed complement of Georgian goblet embracing tables,
      damask linen—

Could you then cross this universe
Time challenge and find the same peace of mind
      traverse
As from "Oak House"—we link with golden gorse
In clouded banks of Brockweir's melodious primrose
      purse:

I pick a yellow garland dyed scarlet wind to mauve—
A small Toadflax honey-mouthed bee roves
With early spur in Campion's scarlet alcoves—
How mossy Saxifrage is linked in love
With Chervil wild shares Cowslip's loving cup:

The hedge beyond fair reach of Parsley—
Herb-Robert pink in wave of Lady Smock ballêt—

I choose in Speedwell's Fingered and Persian's gay
The Columbine to strengthen blues bouquêt:
How lesser Celandine, Marsh Marigold reflect
In May—Repeat in golds Kingcup, contrasting Violet,
Yes! Mellow Rose! Blue, ochre flowers, leaves pressed wet:
Wined foliage and food of lane-long the memory serves
      best . . .

Gloucester, 1976.

A visit to "O Stranger's" life-long friends near Gloucester.

A Prayer in Drought

O ye of little faith Divine
    the waters of the inner mind
O walk barefoot, bare grass to feel
    the soul of raindrop and kneel—
A kneel beside fear's bucket drought
    in realization of Heaven's spout;
Spout ye of renewed faith inquire
    of all elements wealth admire?
O ye of little faith Divine
    in tunnel dark of inner mind
Quell minds cold flood in whispered
    night through channel interflow
Light
Infinite . . .

Written over the period of drought until the first September rains, Elstree. Published in the *Times* and *Post,* October, 1976. In this year the book *Notail at Wesley* was written—a survival story of a family of blackbirds in drought, summer 1976.

156

The Generation Gap

Never the Twain, My Son

Your way and mine
Now poles apart, yours to the nuclear fission's brilliant art,
Higher degrees; scientific whys, universal rise
From cloistered thesis, ancient archives, historic walls.
The atoms prize
Deep theory, strong thirsts the learned halls
From knowledge; the complex, precise chart.

We tryst in bright stars . . .
Proud, cloudless azure skies where calculus in memory parts
The haze of bluebells
Beamed myriad briars pink dawns of mushroomed skies
Red sand drawn fine
Thin, stencilled lines mark time
Your way and mine . . .

***

Your way and mine
Julian, my grandson, pointing to the moon with grubby fist,
Here snuggled on the garden seat in tryst:
"I picked these for you today . . . "
The bluebell haze
Bunch now at our feet
We tryst in bright stars
"We go to California, Nanny
But I will not forget . . . "
Thin, stencilled lines are time
Until the ocean crossed
Your way and mine . . .

Published in *Poetry Panorama,* 1971 (to Dr. R. B. Duffey). Part 2, 1976,
Stroud.

The Organ Stops

*(In memory of my aunt, who was church organist until her
illness and death)*

A citadel she keeps
tomb where her heart is barred from rest . . .
a running stave past day which breaks
in vibrant half with patient's tasks
as unreal as forgotten ivories.
When climbing homes' last stair
oppressive incubus sigh of spirit weans,
towers to hospital clean.

This citadel she keeps
her groping eyes stopped in natural keys
distress of coughs, awakening disease
grim siege in a heart's cave and flames
singe to aching brain:
Circumvents all night in curious whispers
so grievous deep the wash in well
those ivory wounds where no wounds dwell:

Yes! She still believed in God . . .
Yet . . . when did God hear? Sunday conceded
now in her hell tarried
cramped in earthly choirs, the piped
thrusts of calmer youth fence in refrain:
Of citadel she keeps
His bitter seraphim
for beauty laughed once upon her truths

as ointment on spoils
where midnight glow worms shine
and she is left the longue haleine—
the chord lost in hunt of nurses' eyes.
Fox in a lair upon a foreign field,
horn of drawn-down blinds.

THE ORGAN STOPS

the Siegfried March silent, confused
between the sublime . . .

Charing, 1977.

"Wonderful poem will find a place in one of our magazines," Robin
Gregory, editor, *Poetry International,* 1978. "Well crafted, full of interest
and revealing love," *Envoi,* 1978. Runner-up Stroud Festival, 1978 (comp.).

159

Fingers in Time

My Grandmother's First Grandchild

Frail
        Spidery hands that once had rocked her cradle
        webs now that held the love of sons
        and spun the threads of gold imagination
            into small hearts
        and held at bosom's warmth
        the tiny suckling tongue—
            if they could only speak
        in wisdom they are tortured
        from age enriched and loved by world they loved
        and now with added generation
            will wipe away the tears
        in silent admiration
        to feel the soft caress of a great-grandchild's
            hand . . .

Published in *Pilgrimage,* 1972. Read on B.B.C., Scotland, 1972.

A Ring of Amethyst

(With the death of my grandmother)

I transfused, tuned to the warm heliotrope
—laced water music of your room, hope

in calm waltz of sunlit steps as three will pledge
—you with me on black leather Bible's deckle edge . . .

in a living tuning fork of afternoon
—soft quietness rests in contrast of scarlet born

kitten's new mirth: your mirrored reflection
—the slight stroke counterpanes webbed hand in grape-vein:

black cat stirs swiftly from the splintering hearth
—and your loved page flickers worn with "guns before butter" thief

of honey flows from Rupert Brooke's "Granchester"
—drops on your harplike fingers, labors on crochêt . . .

kitten climbs to a blue dust jungle of aspidestra
—your pillows starched halo of hair white-spider

as shot silk into our spire of cathedral descant
—in Eternity's explosion vigilant—

the purest echo in solitaire glare of Death's briefest moment

transfused in a flame-burst of your ring amethyst . . .

Emily Jane Daniel was age ninety-four when she died.

161

A Ladder to Summer

An Altar Vase in Oban Cathedral

Tall gladioli spires
    in laddered climb
bearing a soft green of tender rungs
    in a proud reach of buds
a waxen touch as of angel's tongues.

Petals as lips frame the fanfare
    in laddered climb
bearing the softer altar light, fade
    and glow of heightened pain
of beauty bowed with jade.

The phenomena to summer toils
    in laddered climb
now is her crowned reward
    salute from the dormant cold,
throb and pulse of golden bulb:

Where salve of blood red petal-fall
    in laddered climb
how tender bloom
    humble flower of crimson
towers in strength at Communion rail
    God given from soil . . .

Although the poem was partially composed when the author arrived first in Oban, 1968, I would like it to be followed by "Harvest." It then bears the fruitful thought of a "laddered climb" when at the time of entering the cathedral it was as tower of strength in an aisle of fears . . . and tears.

Harvest

To give:
      To give of ourselves and not to hold
      the priceless joys of giving of our best,
      to feel the need of others where the cold
      of sorrow runs through our own tears and halts
      their suffering: turning through tears fond smiles
To bless.

To gain:
      World gain is ours to lose, life's incomplete
          in gain
      in real understanding, guiding, lightening the path
      depending on His guidance as sunshine after rain,
      to pray and open all the heart strings is the key
          to laugh
      from happiness and peace which comes from prayer—
To care.

To help:
      To live to give our best, the recompense of giving
      from a heart that's hurt and reaps its own rewards,
      to heal the wounds of others by our loving
      in kindness, thoughtfulness and find our own strength
          flower
      in gifts of nature; silence, calm endurance
      from others kindly words these priceless gifts
          not power
A calm from storm!

Published in *Poetry,* 1972. Recommended by Robert Armstrong, February, 1976: " . . . amongst others I like your poem 'Harvest' very much." " . . . very pleasing work," Sir John Betjeman, June 10, 1976.

Thought taken from Psalm 126, verse 5: "They that sow in tears shall reap in joy."

O Stranger

(Part 2)

By Special License

Yes! You belong to summer new
  Four-year rains bore teardrops, too—

The long searching song now rests
  in a mist of balm fragrant violets

Pinned to your lapel and heart
  in throb of full-leaf; contrast stark

The glistening white of my miniature cake-ice
  sharing a crystal bowl in violet confidence!

The journey new of wedded fold
  dress "Wesley's" trees in rippled cloud

Where wedding ring is old:
  Georgian and ruby-red

Delight, for though, "O Stranger,"
  You have caught my wing in water—

I will reach up in outward flight
  soundless as a butterfly your wife—

At Elstree, April, 1978.

The book *Butter in the Buttercups* is dedicated to "the Knight on the White
Charger." In part 3, poem 1, line 3: "Now FOUR: how pleased we leave
troy-weight dust for Wonderland's Green!" (1976)

To Hold a Wild Bird in the Hand

Infinity

LISTEN—I call him "Whitewing,"
grown from the hand of a year's rearing, feeding
of bird wild in the fullest constancy of trusting—

I call him "Whitewing," a fledged blackbird
calls from nestling in "Family Tree" wings bird
wild to flutter under winter's snowed hedge, spring's
    Paradise shared—

for Paradise was never lost; secretly is just, long
hidden between black feathered raiment in dormant song;
a loyal, deeper sensitivity of quiet where seventy-nine's
    snow prolongs

to sunburst upon a black-laced trellis to hold a wild bird high
in twigged and frosted morning flowers a silhouette in sky,
crimson in flushed bud of February sun, to my descant's why—
O why! Could one minute, compassionate, and crystal throat
compare to all daybreaks in trilled, beaked notes—
contained in vibrant echoed song in streams of time remote?

I call him "Whitewing"—LISTEN
He holds the dreams of youth, wild histories of man—
Listen and hear perfection in one note of his allotted span,
To hold a wild bird in the hand.

The garden at Wesley. Written when living in Elstree. Published in "Spotlight," Sunday *Durango Herald.* Chosen by Dr. John Tapia, chairman, Dept. of Foreign Languages, Fort Lewis College, Colorado, October, 1980.

"The Bloom": *Anthology International,* 1981. Dr. Amal Ghose, Tagore Institute of Creative Writing. Five poems (from *Wings of Sound*) including "To Hold a Wild Bird in the Hand." Other titles not known at present.

Claustrophobia

(As visualized in early morning at the hairdresser's)

Only her three tender years
  of blue-white nylon frills,
as charming in her "embroiderie anglais"

dress—I; watching born to an age
  of "petticoat" anglaise, a sage
solemn-faced, starched-white age—

dripping as September mists
  she cries and tucks her petal frills
with thumb perpetually numb; sucks

tranquil on her rose bud tongue,
  where boredom cruel for young is long—
claustrophobia scents waft strong—

amid spray: "Did I not hear Dr. Martland
  is in extensive care?" A strand
wet of my own washed hair tight in a band—

layered beneath the plastic globe of dryer,
  where gossip mixed is mist whipped;
eschewed, lip read: a voice here?

But see the petal-lip pucker
  as the steel scissors snip—erase a smile;
blur her eyes, tresses were erased long as Mother's—

in eyebrow raise: "Suits her the Grecian style?!"
  Now with the deaf and dumb, curled and numb
her inner center whirled of new-age girl—
        sobs her twin sister . . .

New Romney, 1980.

The author has now returned to New Romney and in the house of birth
with "O Stranger."

166

On Wings of Sound

Poem 1

"Now Hold the Sound"
The Cinque Ports Poets Annual Dinner
December 6, 1980

NOW HOLD THE SOUND . . .
    of purest magic transpose the muse,
        in a strong rhythmical equation and vibration—
        backing of drums: the talented poets
            of many nations . . .
                In unison their voices here infuse:

Collected at "The Plumtree House" true magic of a moment's key
    when turned reveals the first child anxiously to read
        her poem:
            So tenderly as her years about her "Snowman"—
            She questions reverently: "You can't leave me

Now with wounds that cannot mend?!"
    Ten children read their verses . . .
        and from age six to eighty-six the age converses
        as the wine—merriment and dinner of the
            Cinque Ports Poets blend:

Mingle from the grand introduction jeu d'esprit
    a reading by a boy student from his recent letter
        sent to me:
            Containing all his thoughts in deep sincerity:
                " . . . I feel quite proud you've chosen me

To meet Howard Sergeant, M.B.E.
    Thank you for this moment rare—
        Your Annual Dinner I can share . . ."
        A genuine "Brotherhood and Peace Through Poetry"
Poems from *The Field of Buttercups* in magic—
    Members who in turn have joined in poesie
        Now listen with a rapt attention to my *Cameo*
            of poems
                sent from overseas—to my speech and Howard's
                reading magnetic—

167

Glowing magic of the candlelight success of a December night
evaluates moonshine of faces where love has winged
    her way:
    Through countryside—over deeper oceans—
    Tying the bond that BELONGS TO SOUND in swift
    Flight . . .
        A spirit-wing and toast of the
        —CINQUE PORTS POETS—

"NOW HOLD THE SOUND" from "To the West Indies; "a revolving stage," from *On Wings of Sound*, Poem 2.

Survival

He ploughed the darkened furrow of the night—
  This monster; gruesome, black, appalling as foresight—

Of the moment's impact where no stars shine—
  And shattering nerve in stony silence of the after-crime—

I shudder where the butterflies of belly cry
  Look at my husband; still and staring straight decry

"Are you alright, darling?" a dry, choked sob, whisper *"Thank
    God"*—
And then the devil took my tongue in rod

Of abuse I stampede; hurl back at the unknown driver,
  Who bunched, weeping at his wheel—a frightened player

On the speeding stage of life! His remorse on loss of control
  On a bend; wicked, of a marsh road rolling, sees not the bare
               SOUL
In pity murmurs, "It was my fault, I know"—
  "But look at my car,"   repeats in torrent thrice
          "IT WAS NEW"

"Look at my husband then, you b--- fool
  He could be dead; mangled, and I and you! Your woeful
    sobbing cruel . . ."

               ***

Traffic; noise, police, ambulance where all stars shine—
  Radiant and God-given: Ourselves—we hold again the hidden
    Lamp of Time

December 29, 1980. This and the following two poems written after the accident.

Exactly five years since "A Rustle in the Rain." " . . . as Death sans fear one hears the turn of tide" as in poem "Symmetry," again the transformation given by Light.

I quote from poem "The Cinque Ports Poets Dinner," "Friends, please slow the pace/Remember our Fred's poetic epitaph . . . on this blackbird cock."

It was on this same road in 1974 a transitive thought was expressed. In 1980 an accident occurred between the Sussex and Kent borders.

The Mute Swan Song

With beauty and grace—
Resting behind porcelain and plate—
  In this day and age my collector's guide would say—
    "Value more than fifty pounds today?"
I turned musing away, Christmas pension complete!
  Ten minutes pass when my son with swan on trembling palm
    A smile wreathing his face in calm:
      "Have you seen this, Mother? It is Belleek!"
The smile returned, a torment in my cheek . . .
  "I know!" Unmistakable and sleek.

  The Mute Swan
Light . . . feather light in beauty and all grace
  Reflected on the higher lights of counterspace—
    Mirrored, I inquire: "Why is it then so cheap?"
      "Ten pounds?" My son held her beauty bosom high
To neon light . . . perfect in flight, oblique
  A finger and thumb seen through finest porcelain—
    And her most graceful neck   ●
    In swoop of time bore a minute hair's crack!
"Yes, of course, a blindman would appreciate that in palaquin,"
  The assistant's turn to smile awry.

    "You may have it then for nine"—
The Mute Swan with tissue and newsprint I wrap in a basket of new
    jest,
  Now only temporary her beautiful and solitary rest—
    With beauty and grace! A tranquil face
With my mind in calculation of glazed cabinet: her permanent
    place—
    With Worcester all period, Derby Crown and Dresden store
      From Great-Grandmother's, Mother's miniature collection
      galore—
    The cabinet brims *yet* could hold one more?

                    ***

    Four? Maybe five hours in a nightmare maelstrom pass—
Time an indelible morass—
  Husband, family—I, mentally crushed and heart-sore
    Home with trepidation the Mute Swan we eventually table-
    toss—

Will she sing as sweetly as Only at Death's door?
  With beauty and new grace
    Antiquity replace?

The car in accident is "written-off," indeed
  She was then reclining quietly serene at my stoic feet—
    But now the hairline crack is hidden twice as sweet—
    INTACT from driving maniac with break-neck speed—
  In retrospect shall gaze and glaze her long, saffron beak
    In silence
        and with strong companions keep . . .

December 29, 1980.

"Belleek"—a very fine porcelain made in Ireland, said to take its gloss from
the use of the scales of the herring.

Symmetry of the New . . .

Now—in galaxy, may all stars shine—dance
  Where a moon in velvet rapture calms—
Cradles my first night to acquiesce . . .

"I think toward you"—
Saith the Lord—"Thoughts of Peace
And not of evil to:
  Give you an expected end"—
"By a New Wave of Living
  Forsaken not"—Resurrected
The Rainbow has an end?
  From piercing cry
From portrait of Death—a Friend . . .

***

Such blossom—the sungold of a January
  Marsh day! I listen—hear
In heart's desire a solitary

  Spark from fire . . .
The lamp lit and room ablaze
  When a hundred Christmas cards acquire

Their warmest greeting; vibrant, new—
  Each an individual, beloved portrait of poet—
Friend in gallery attained, world-melodious
    Brotherhood on view . . .

New Romney, 1981.

The friends of poem "On Leaving One's Friends," line 12. 1968?

Renewal of the Cinque Ports Poets on return in 1975 to New Romney. The commencement of an anthology to commemorate for all time the "International Year of the Child." A book entitled *A Field of Buttercups* with poems from worldwide. Contributors junior and senior.

Ivory Dark

Only then shall I sleep . . .
with this mad moonlight
woven tight around my fleeced heart;
nightjars shall have no calling
seashore alone
shall catch the bell-tide dawning
break in distress from ivory dark,
smoke-tongue of flame
the everyday miracle of love and rain:

Only then shall I sleep
In the flowered meadow—
call of the ivory dark
when you speak my name . . .

New Romney, 1975.

Published in the *Community News,* December, 1980, and "Spotlight," *Sunday Durango Herald,* Colorado, October, 1980.

Fragrant Moonbeams

As fragrance of champagne
flows in long, silken flame
the tresses of autumn cage
burnt amber in the shade . . .

Soft tendrils trace
a perfume of sweet pines
so wafts a deep forest's rest
anatomy of vines,

deep stress of purple heath;
heather, quick thyme
jest of a last wild rose
anile in gray crease of rest—

ferns lace-warm to a pheasant's breast—
as night dew blest moon's furrowed brow,
sad ivory eye in braided yellow
sparkling beam . . . bubbling stream
of champagne

mellowed, fragrant
bottled brae of clear white wine!

Written in 1970, in rough form, produced as selection of verses by request of Dr. John Tapia and published in "Spotlight," Sunday *Durango Herald,* Colorado, September, 1980. Published as Guest Poetry Editors' to the West Sussex Federation of Town's Women's Guilds in their Award Poems Edition of 1981.

The fragrance of night in a northern forest. Highlands of Scotland.

To My Granddaughters

To Rebecca

Deep violets, brimming magical eyes
    her smile beams warm
as blithe spring sunshine rays an april morn . . .
    Her honey-dewed three years
blossom in sweet surprise, raised questioning eyes:
    "Are you sad, too, Nanny,
that today you have to up, and go away?"

    Flower tufts my fragrant sleep,
far, warm cry of golden moment keeps—
    Heart's glad tears of delight
in winter-sweet bouquêt, a soft-clad purple light . . .

To a Flower

To you . . . sweet JULIA
    remembrance of a child . . .
dainty as forget-me-nots
    true wish of spring, flower wild
in blue eyes which smile?
    Stealth of petal-soft skin
your hand in mine . . .
    Your laughter in my mind—akin
        as water ripples
            trills in its flow—love
Sparkles through your charms
        sunrays
            in breeze
                that wafts
            your fairy curls
upon a swing
    of birthday's soft remembering . . .

Published in *Pilgrimage*, 1972. Reviewed as poem "To My Mother"—to
be published by Dr. Allison Johnn-St. Johnn, New York.

The two poems were written in exile and were in retrospect of meeting the
children. Julia is the "Buttercup" of *Butter in the Buttercups*.

175

Outpatients

"I came at half-past one . . ." the patient sighs
an old man, shrunken eye sockets and his coat outsize—
It seemed . . . the footfalls reminiscent as on church stone
In shuffle, whispers between the lady patients known.
A Communion rail where congregational eye and ear
Transmute still in pew await definitely to hear
The minister for their health . . . a sermon rare
Dwelling behind the doctor's trepid gaze, their fear . . .

He understands—nods like God to appease—
Displease? Selects the pills—the patient pales—
A door secretly opens and unushered in a frail
And weary man who's path Death surely hails?

. . . quietly still they wait, laughter becomes a second place—
Melancholy in brilliant neon light their eyes raise,
Then soften to the Book once read, eyes still chastise—
THEIR TURN? Sigh as their turn as Lot's wife to take
          their only road long as Fate—
For now the longer lesson learns in Cross and Creed . . .
"Nurse will take your blood . . ."
     "I BELIEVE—"
They; mesmerized and filed footsteps cold as on church stone
Whispers between the patients now unknown—
A trolley rattles with the tea-time crocks:
"WHY?" in hesitant voice, "WHY was I told to come at four
     o'clock?"
"Tell me?" the blind and wizened women questions between coughs,
Closes the door softly, her white stick
          tap—
               tapping—
                    disconsolate
          Down
               the corridor
               of fugitive
               LOST . . .

The William Harvey Hospital, 1980.

176

Last Journey

(To My Mother)

In Love of God
  This the reality,
    pearl—quiet beauty in the Majesty of Heaven,
  in midnight's solemn massed gaze of perfect sleep
    in Eternities' shadowed pools, her loved eyes sink deep—
  into their shrine of leaven light
    where butterflies retreat . . .

In this faith's naked sapphire sea; as visions stay,
  where night has tuned dark eyes upon my lost star's way . . .

She'll peep between far honey stars
  to rest her soul upon still clouds of midday . . .
Where love of sleep from pain, to love of light will be
  her sanctuary between.

Although fond eyes now dimmed in sight,
  Blue Light, where part of day is part of night
    and knowledge gleams!

Published in *Pilgrimage,* 1972. Reading given at the "Little Mull Theatre."
Reviewed by John Smith, then editor, *Poetry Review.* Also by June Chisholm
and Iain Crighton-Smith. Reviewed and to be published by Dr. Allison
Johnn-St. Johnn.

My mother, Gertrude Clara Gower (Daniel: married Beecher Daniel), the
Guthrie-Gowers of Sutherland and of Tring. Herts.

177

On Wings of Sound

Summer's Storm in Oban Bay
(Poem 2)

White arrowed rain
where spume pirouettes
as white nymphs cadence
in ballet foam, a gay ballerina's dance
entranced above a bottle green

revolving stage,

gray anchors to a weeping wall
in a back cloth gleaming orchestra and stalls:

Heaven shakes clenched fists
to toss a ball, a sun a moment long:
rare mood is caught her ballerina's fly
in sunbeams purple and pink-fingered sky
The choreography plucks wild
lyrics transmute on plumes of cloud:
Gulls pipe, high-fluted notes wheel in pride
with wicked waves on hungry billowed

TIDE

Creeps crown of blue upon an ochre tress
Storm coils above a pique of trembling serpents
Curtsies—accepts
a prima donna's waltz
her theme of praise

ON WINGS OF SOUND

Grand rainbowed FINALE
of lyric waves
White —   —rain

CURTAIN

Other Books by Stella Browning

Pilgrimage and Other Poems

Published by L.L.E. Anthology 1972 (o.p.)
London & America   500 copies

Editor: HORIZON

Published by the Author for Cinque Ports
Poets   1973-75 (o.p.)
                                    2,000 copies

Butter in the Buttercups

Published by the Author Parts 1 & 2 1977
Second Edition: May/77
Third Edition: Spring/78 with Part 3
First Edition: Spring/80 Hardcover

Butter in the Buttercups
With:
Notail at Wesley

Published by the Author
December 1977
Blackbird and Wildlife in
Hertfordshire garden

The Adventures of Hoodie
the Crow

Published in April 1980
Wildlife in the Mountains of N.W. Scotland
fully illustrated

Stranger Than Fiction
Part I
"Childhood"

Prose in progress

A Field of Buttercups

Poems for Children, by Children and
about Children; international contributions
An anthology for Cinque Ports Poets
to commemorate the International
Year of the Child. 1983

New Publication by
Aquila Press (Dr. J. C. R. Green)
entitled "A Romney Marsh
Tapestry"

Calendar of poetry including historical,
topical, personal poems for 1982. Publica-
tion in 1983. Foreword by Dr. Allison
Johnn-St. Johnn.